Excluded from School

Excluded from School exposes the reasons why, despite many national and local initiatives, large numbers of children continue to tax the education system to such a degree that they become permanently excluded from school.

Sue Rendall and Morag Stuart draw on their experience in psychology and education to demonstrate the need for a more thorough exploration of the underlying root causes of the problem. Based on a systemic framework, their approach allows the inclusion of a vast range of possible contributory factors: within the child, within the family, within the school, and within the complex interrelations between these three systems. By demonstrating the need for inter-discipline and inter-agency collaboration, the authors succeed in presenting a persuasive challenge to the blame culture which exists between schools, parents and educational professionals and policy-makers in relation to school exclusion.

The original research presented here, along with the inclusion of the experiences of children, parents and teachers, provides a valuable new perspective on the problem of school exclusions that will be welcomed by all professionals working in this field.

Sue Rendall is a Consultant Child and Educational Psychologist and Director of Educational Psychology Training at The Tavistock Clinic, London. She is a Chartered Educational Psychologist, and Fellow of The University of Essex.
Morag Stuart is Professor of Psychology at The Institute of Education, University of London.

Excluded from School

Systemic Practice for Mental Health and Education Professionals

Sue Rendall & Morag Stuart

Routledge
Taylor & Francis Group

LONDON AND NEW YORK

First published 2005 by Routledge
27 Church Road, Hove, East Sussex, BN3 2FA

Simultaneously published in the USA and Canada
by Routledge
270 Madison Avenue, New York, NY 10016

Routledge is an imprint of the Taylor & Francis Group

Typeset in Times by
RefineCatch Ltd., Bungay, Suffolk
Printed and bound in Great Britain by
TJ International Ltd, Padstow, Cornwall
Paperback cover design by Lisa Dynan

This publication has been produced with paper manufactured
to strict environmental standards and with pulp derived from
sustainable forests.

British Library Cataloguing in Publication Data
A catalogue record for this book is available
from the British Library

Library of Congress Cataloging-in-Publication Data
Rendall, Sue.
    Excluded from school : systemic practice for mental health
and education professionals / Sue Rendall and Morag Stuart.
        p. cm.
    Includes bibliographical references and index.
    ISBN 1–58391–847–7 (hbk) – ISBN 1–58391–848–5 (pbk)
    1. Student expulsion – England – London Metropolitan Area –
Case studies.   2. Educational psychology – Case studies.
I. Stuart, Morag.   II. Title.
LB3089.4G7R46 2005
371.5′43′0942—dc22   2004025868

ISBN 1-58391-847-7 (hbk)
ISBN 1-58391-848-5 (pbk)

This book is dedicated to Gordon and Bob for their love, support and patience.

Contents

List of illustrations

Tables

Figures

Chapter 1

The wider social and political context

Setting the scene

In this book, we describe a study that we carried out in an attempt to increase understanding of the factors that lead to some children being permanently excluded from school. The desire to design and implement such a study arose initially from the clinical experience of the first author in her work as an educational psychologist employed by a local education authority, which involved working with pupils who had been excluded from school. The cases of two pupils in particular caused her to wonder what it was about these two young people, who were similar in some ways but markedly different in others in terms of their educational and medical histories, their family circumstances and the ethos of the two schools from which they were excluded, that had led to them being excluded. This in turn raised in her a curiosity about the circumstances of other children who had been excluded from school, and a desire to understand whether and in what ways children who become permanently excluded from school might differ from children of the same age, gender, ethnicity and school who have not been excluded.

There were clear and obvious differences between these two pupils, whom we shall call Nadine and Richard. Nadine was female, white, from a working-class family, living in a council owned property with her younger sister and divorced mother. Richard was male, black African-Caribbean, from a professional family, living with his younger brother and both parents in their own private house. Upon further enquiry, some similarities became apparent. Both were the elder of two children in the family. Both had well above average general ability, although each school from which they were excluded had described them as being of average ability but underachieving. Both were excluded during their first year in the secondary school.

Other similarities included both having medical conditions which had required hospitalisation throughout their lives. Nadine suffered from epilepsy and diabetes, Richard suffered from severe asthma and eczema. There had been considerable family conflict in each family. Nadine's parents were divorced and Richard reported that his parents constantly argued and his mother had said that she was going to leave. Both pupils had been referred to the educational psychologist and local child guidance centre, but both had been excluded from school before receiving an appointment. Both pupils blamed their exclusion and difficulties entirely upon things beyond their control. Nadine blamed her exclusion on 'stupid teachers not understanding [her] medical condition' and Richard blamed 'racist teachers and other kids' for his difficulties. Neither was able to offer any suggestions as to what they might have done differently which might have helped their situation.

These two cases highlighted for us the complicated aspects involved in attempting to understand what contributes to some pupils being excluded from school. We have met many children who appear to come from situations and conditions similar to Nadine and Richard, but who do not get excluded from school. For this reason it was important for us to include a matched comparison group of non-excluded children in the present study, in an attempt to clarify why this might be so.

Working directly with permanently excluded children has reinforced our opinion that there is merit in taking a holistic model of enquiry when trying to understand how these permanent exclusions came about. Behaviour only acquires meaning and can only be understood within the context in which it occurs. Children do not exist in a vacuum, but within many complex interrelating systems. They develop as individuals with their own personal understandings, belief systems and ways of making sense of the world: we will refer to this as the 'within-child' system. This development happens in the immediate context of their families, which we refer to as the 'within-family' system, that is influenced by family members, family histories, beliefs and values and family scripts and experiences. Children's development also takes place in the context of the institutions of the wider society, with school being of major importance here. We refer to this as the 'within-school' system, which is in turn influenced by school structures, ethos, values and beliefs, legislation and society's notion of the function and place of schools, teachers and education.

Our study therefore embraces a systemic model of enquiry, the theoretical bases of which are described in detail in Chapter 2. The study uses both quantitative and qualitative data in order to elicit a rich picture of the complexities involved in the interrelating systems studied. We have used measures such as psychometric tests, that lend themselves to quantitative analysis using statistical tests. We have also used semi-structured interviews and questionnaires to identify recurring themes from the stories that pupils, parents and teachers told us, and which lend themselves to qualitative analysis. This dual approach to data collection and analysis provides a more realistic and deeper picture of the experiences and underlying conflicts and dilemmas that exist for pupils, parents and teachers. We believe that the first step towards preventing permanent exclusions from school is to have the fullest possible understanding of the circumstances in which they occur.

We were also constantly mindful of the ethical issues that inevitably arise in the course of a study such as the one we set out to conduct. For example, from the onset of the research engagement all pupils and parents were told that taking part in our study would not help to reverse the decision to exclude nor to find them another school to attend. However, where pupils, parents or teachers clearly had needs that needed to be addressed, we were able to refer them on to appropriate agencies. In writing up the study in book form, we have been careful to use pseudonyms throughout and to ensure that we maintain the confidentiality of children, parents, schools and teachers.

In 1991 when Nadine and Richard were permanently excluded from their schools, there appeared to be little public concern or debate about exclusions from school, although shortly after this time educationalists, and later politicians, began to express concerns about the numbers of school exclusions, the costs to the public purse and the effects which pupils out of school might be having upon local communities, society and themselves. The remainder of this chapter first presents national and local data about exclusion from school, and the debates that have arisen in this context. We then give a brief overview of the study we undertook, and outline the way in which we have structured our material in the chapters that follow.

The national context

Although children have probably been expelled, suspended, or excluded from schools since schools began, exclusion has been of particular concern to educationalists, government, the media and the public at large since the early 1990s. Prior to 1990 there was some academic interest in and professional concern about the reasons why some pupils faced and experienced exclusion (for example, Galloway *et al.* 1982; McLean 1987; McManus 1987). Reliable data on permanent exclusions has been obtained only since 1996, from Annual Schools' Census returns made by schools to the DfEE in January each year. However, there was anxiety from the early 1990s onwards that the number of temporary and permanent exclusions from schools was rising, and this anxiety was frequently accompanied by claims that structural changes in the ways schools were managed (for example, the decentralisation of power within the education system introduced in the Education Reform Act 1988, which introduced a greater complexity to the tasks of schools and teachers) were not only exacerbating schools' difficulties in meeting the needs of pupils with challenging behaviour, but perhaps reducing their desire or willingness to do so. The subsequent introduction of the National Curriculum, National Literacy and Numeracy Strategies and Performance League Tables reinforced these difficulties, by making academic outcomes the prime focus of education. The development and promotion of emotional well-being, social awareness and inclusion began to be viewed as important only with respect to how they affected academic outcome.

DfES figures published in 2001–2 showed that permanent exclusions had reached an 'unacceptably high' peak of 12,700 (17 pupils in every 10,000) representing a threefold increase between the early and late 1990s. Some of this increase was doubtless due to important changes in the law regarding exclusions from school which came into force in 1994. The category of 'indefinite' exclusion, where pupils were sent home with no indication as to when or under what circumstances they could return to school (which caused great concern to parents, LEAs and educationalists, as often this resulted in pupils getting 'lost' in the system and therefore effectively leaving school prior to the statutory school leaving age) was abolished. This left schools with only two options for excluding pupils: 'fixed term' exclusion, where pupils were sent home for a fixed amount of time, after which they could return to school; or 'permanent' exclusion, when pupils could never return to that school. At this point in time, therefore, schools had either to permanently exclude pupils who had been on 'indefinite' exclusions, or allow them to return to school, with most probably becoming permanently excluded. Since September 1994 the National Union of Teachers (NUT) and the Head Teachers' Association have continued to campaign for the reinstatement of the 'indefinite exclusion' option, arguing that it provides a more flexible option for planning to meet children's educational needs.

Whatever the cause of the sudden upsurge in permanent exclusions, it galvanised the government into setting as a priority the reduction of levels of permanent exclusions. The importance of this priority was emphasised when school exclusions became one of the specific topics to be addressed by the Social Exclusion Policy Unit, launched in 1997 by the Prime Minister, Tony Blair, and reporting directly to him. By 2002, the unit planned to reduce exclusions by one-third, to provide excluded pupils with a full-time timetable within three weeks of exclusion, to provide funds for prevention of school exclusion, to require school performance tables of GCSE results to include all Year 10 exclusions, and for particular attention to be given to looked after children.

Setting and emphasising this as a priority appears at first to have had some effect, with overall levels of permanent exclusion decreasing slightly at first (to 12,300 in 1997–8) followed by a further massive 30 per cent decrease to just over 8300 (11 pupils in every 10,000) in 1999–2000. However, figures have begun to creep up again since then, increasing to 9,500 (12 pupils in every 10,000) by 2001–2. Throughout this period, the vast majority of exclusions (roughly 80 per cent) have been from secondary schools, but pupils attending special schools are the most likely to be excluded, with rates of 36 pupils in every 10,000 excluded from special schools. Pupils with statements of special educational needs (SEN) are also over-represented among the excluded, by a ratio of almost 8:1 during the exclusion peak of 1996–7. Boys are overwhelmingly more likely to be excluded than girls, with a steady 4:1 ratio of boys to girls. Boys are also excluded at younger ages than girls, although for both boys and girls exclusion is most common in 13 and 14 year olds (pupils in Years 9 and 10), with one in every 250 pupils in this age range excluded. Exclusion rates vary by ethnic group as well as by gender, with the highest rates found in black African-Caribbean pupils. Black girls are three times as likely to be excluded as white girls; black boys are twice as likely to be excluded as white boys. Children who are 'looked after' by local authorities are also at increased risk of permanent exclusion from school.

At a National Children's Bureau Conference 'Exclusion – or Inclusion – and the School System' held in February 1997, Robin Squire MP, then Parliamentary Under Secretary of State for Schools, DfEE said:

> Good behaviour and effective discipline are at the heart of school standards. It is vital that schools should have the skills and the support necessary to manage pupil behaviour effectively. There is properly a balance to be struck. We need to ensure that pupils with problems receive effective education and support. But that should not be at the cost of undermining the education of the vast majority of well behaved pupils either because resources are redirected unduly, or because their classes are persistently disrupted . . . We are committed to ensuring that schools are able to deal with behaviour problems as far as possible without having to exclude pupils.

This position is somewhat ambiguous and affords schools and LEAs a degree of flexible interpretation of which many may take the fullest advantage. The difficulty of interpretation lies in such questions as how does a school support challenging pupils and meet their needs without redirecting resources, and what constitutes 'unduly' with respect to such redirection? More often than not it is the tolerance level of the school to manage challenging behaviour that determines whether or not the spirit of Robin Squire's words is adhered to, and whether or not a pupil is excluded. Government rhetoric may sound convincing but is seldom helpful in recognising some of the more subtle challenges which face schools and pupils who are experiencing difficulties.

Indeed, in his presentation to the same conference, David Hart, then General Secretary of the National Association of Head Teachers (NAHT), explained his members' position with regard to the allocation of resources, saying that the overall problem was that of the needs of the many versus the needs of the few, and that the needs of the few to be 'rehabilitated' could not be done 'on the cheap'. He claimed that the introduction of league tables, the consequent general competitiveness between schools, and the need for schools to attract pupils in order to attract funding had all contributed to the increase in exclusions and to the breakdown of necessary systems and partnerships. These factors all serve to lower tolerance levels towards pupils with challenging behaviour. There was now also increased recognition of teachers' rights not to be assaulted or to have their tolerance stretched to breaking point. Furthermore, the introduction and demands of the SEN Code of Practice, within a context of constant debate about, and under funding of, integration and inclusive education, led to difficulties for schools surrounding implementation of the code, and frustration on the part of teachers.

It is clear from this list that changes in the wider system of society are causing changes in the schools and education system which increase the likelihood of producing a subgroup of children who do not 'fit in' and for whom permanent exclusion from school is seen to be the only option. Hart continued to describe the development of 'an education and social underclass', comprising those pupils who are unattractive to schools, either because they are of low educational ability and/or because they present behaviour which is difficult to manage. These pupils are 'unattractive' because they are a drain on schools' financial and time resources. Consequently they often do not have their needs met within the mainstream sector, with mainstream schools believing that specialist provision is more appropriate. The National Association of Head Teachers' view is that it is the combination of reduced tolerance on behalf of schools and governors, combined with a lack of adequate funding, which has led to the increase in excluded pupils. It also subscribes to the view that no pupil should be readmitted to a mainstream school until that school receives additional funding and resources and a favourable pupil report. This suggests that each excluded pupil would need to attend alternative educational provision in order to acquire a favourable pupil report; a suggestion which is at odds with the DfEE view, as presented by Robin Squires, that 'permanently excluded pupils are to be admitted fairly rapidly to another mainstream school'.

The NAHT has advised that the Teacher Training Agency (TTA) should ensure that initial teacher training courses address the need to understand the modern school. As acknowledged by Hart, the introduction of published league tables, Ofsted inspections and the public identification of 'failing schools' provide little incentive for schools to 'hang on' to those pupils who are likely to affect their reputation and public image. Teacher training, especially training to teach in the secondary sector, has tended to be curriculum and subject focused, with little emphasis being placed upon trainee teachers being taught child or adolescent development.

With a new government taking office in 1997, with a mission statement of 'Education, Education, Education', greater emphasis has been placed upon evidence-based practice, outcome measures, performance-related pay for teachers, market forces and raising achievement. Parsons (1999) highlights some of the diverse and contradictory aims of education in the UK, and describes the tensions between individual development, vocational training and discipline. Parsons argues that where societies, and in particular educationalists and politicians, place their value affects the development of policies which can lead to the prevention or encouragement of the withdrawal of some children from the formal education system through their permanent exclusion from school. Parsons suggests the following descriptions (presented here as Table 1.1) of a continuum of approaches to the six functions of education in the UK, which he identifies not as moral positions but rather as constructs to help understanding.

Parsons argues that where schools position themselves on the continuum from a social democratic and humanist approach to a controlling approach affects the likelihood of school policies and practices which favour the exclusion from school of the most challenging and 'different' pupils. Parsons's model proposes that the further to the right of this model that a school moves, the more likely the ethos of that school will favour the achievement of goals such as high standards in basic skills and more traditional curriculum subjects, and a controlled school population. Such an ethos presents as being less tolerant of difference, with a greater expectation of conformity and runs counter to the goals of inclusion, recognition

Table 1.1 Continuum of six functions of education

Function	Social democratic humanist	Classical controlling
Custodial	Benign and nurturing	Controlling and limiting
Civilising	Democratising / humanising	Subjugating and inducting
National identity	Open and questioning	Closed and nationalistic
Skilling	Generic and flexible	Specific and fixed
Credentialling	Egalitarian and communitarian	Elitist and competitive
Public knowledge	Conjectural and open	Received and authoritarian

and celebration of diversity and opportunities for pupils to develop responsibility for and own their own behaviour. The introduction of the National Curriculum and league tables has not encouraged the latter ethos to develop and has led to many schools giving a lower priority to the pastoral role of schools, including the opportunity to address individual children's strengths in areas other than those traditional subjects. Parsons's model is concerned exclusively with the political and social context of education, which impacts greatly upon all pupils who are educated within the state education system. We return to these themes when discussing the concept and impact of school ethos in Chapter 5.

In 1994, the Association of Educational Psychologists (AEP) responded to the DfEE Draft Circular 10/94 'Exclusions from School'. This response is worthy of detailed reporting as it highlights some of our concerns regarding steps that are, or rather are not, being taken to understand why more schools are excluding more pupils:

> The circular does not attempt to address the reasons why rates of exclusions have mushroomed in recent years . . . there appears to be a growing body of alienated, disaffected young people who feel devalued in the current system . . . the establishment of a market economy and competition between schools has some ineluctable consequences. One of these is the devaluing of certain groups of children and young people, and placing schools under pressure to exclude them . . . the exclusion problem keeps being moved around, rather than tackled at its source . . . there is little indication of any positive outcomes of exclusion . . . for many pupils the effects are long term and thus not appreciated, and have little influence or impact in changing behaviour.

This response was disappointing in that, whilst being sound in content and argument, it refers to 'the current system' only in the context of society, making no direct reference to the interrelating systems of within-child, within-school and within-family factors, which we suggest warrant further comment and investigation. To date, the interactions and interrelationships among these systems that can influence whether or not, and which, children become permanently excluded from school have not been investigated.

Some recent studies have identified family stress, special educational needs and socio-economic deprivation (Parsons 1995a; Hayden 1997) as common circumstances that surround pupils who have been excluded from school. Brodie and Berridge (1994) comment that excluded pupils do share a number of characteristics in terms of gender and family background, but they warn that, whilst there is merit in acknowledging these common characteristics, it would be inappropriate to conclude that excluded pupils form an entirely homogeneous group: 'The problems these young people displayed were often highly individual in nature and their family backgrounds exceedingly complex.' Whilst the present study acknowledges that it is not possible to identify a truly homogeneous group of excluded pupils any more than this is possible with any group of human beings, there are significant patterns of background, school and family circumstances and conditions, and individual characteristics that can help to identify pupils who may be vulnerable to getting themselves into difficulties likely to lead to exclusion from school. However, there are also many pupils who present similar profiles, yet have not been excluded from school. By employing a matched comparison group the present study seeks to identify more subtle differences between the two groups.

Although the present study does not concern itself with the financial costs of exclusion from school, it is relevant to refer to the Parsons *et al.* (1994) study which considered the financial cost of excluding primary aged pupils. The authors concluded that the tangible financial costs to parents were significant in two of the eleven cases of the study, and that it is important to consider the recurring costs that may ensue in the longer term if substantial intervention is not provided early. Parsons concludes that secondary schools are likely to face problems with these children, child and family health are likely to suffer and require costly medical treatment, engaging in criminal activity is a distinct probability and the longer term problems of adjustment can be predicted into adulthood. The knock-on effects of such activity is expensive in terms of both financial implications and individual health.

Maintaining children in school and diagnosing and meeting their needs may cost less than the estimated £3000 plus per year that is spent on providing excluded children with alternative, often part-time, education. The quality of service received by these children and their families will be immeasurably better at the time, and the prospects of avoiding later problems are greater.

The local context

We carried out our study in a single local education authority in Greater London. In every respect, with the exception of 'looked after children', the local context within which this study is situated is similar to the national picture. When investigating the possible reason for the absence of 'looked after' children from the randomly selected group of excluded children taking part in the present study, the only explanation which seemed reasonable is that there are very small numbers of children being looked after by the local authority, and those children were either in long-term foster homes, foster homes outside the borough or were placed in 52-week residential schools, jointly funded by the LEA and social services.

In 1993–4, at the beginning of our study, there were 75 permanently excluded pupils and 1077 'other' exclusions, from a total school population of 32,926 (3.5 per cent of the school population). Of those children permanently excluded, 64 were male and 11 female (a 6:1 ratio of boys to girls, compared with the DfEE ratio of 5:1 for 1991). In this local context, the two largest ethnic minority groups within the total school population are Turkish and African-Caribbean. Turkish children make up 7 per cent of the total school population, and 3 per cent of the excluded pupil population. African-Caribbean children make up 5 per cent of the total school population, and 10 per cent of the permanently excluded population. Clearly, gender and ethnicity aspects of excluded pupils are important, but the present study will take account of them rather than focus upon them, as there are already several research projects that have specifically addressed these aspects (Cohen *et al.* 1994).

Permanent exclusion figures for this LEA reached a peak in the academic year 1997–8, with a total of 89. Of these, 75 were excluded from secondary schools, 5 from special schools and 10 from primary schools. Figures for the academic year 1998–9 report 77 permanent exclusions, of which 72 were from secondary schools, none from special schools and 5 from primary schools. These figures show a small decrease compared with the previous year, particularly in the primary and special sectors. The small reduction in permanent exclusions is to be welcomed, although we interpret this more as a slowing down in the rise of exclusions rather than an overall decrease in the numbers, as the 1998–9 figures are still higher than the 1993–4 figures. There continues to be an over-representation in the exclusion of black pupils, and boys.

Whilst we were carrying out our study, a number of initiatives were set up to prevent exclusions from school. These include projects funded through the DfEE Standards Funds programme, where the DfEE highlights areas of priority for which LEAs can bid. LEAs are required to match fund these projects. Given the significant amount of financial and professional efforts involved in recent initiatives, one might have expected a greater reduction in the numbers of permanently excluded pupils. This suggests that more money is not the only solution to the quest to reduce exclusions and keep children in a system of productive, useful, enjoyable and rewarding education. We return to this issue in the final chapter of this book. It was clear to us that an attempt to understand some of the more complex issues around this group of excluded children who are deemed to be uneducable within the mainstream or even special education sector was long overdue. Such attempts would seem to be in direct contrast to popular political opinion as expressed in the mid-1990s by the then Prime Minister, John Major, who suggested that we should understand less and condemn more.

Despite the growing body of research and literature which attempts to address the hard data, trends, reasons and implications regarding pupils excluded from school, it seems to us that in order to make any difference to what is acknowledged as a serious social problem, there is a need to understand not only the procedural and political processes around exclusions, but also the emotional and psychological processes. The vast majority of currently available literature on school exclusions is focused upon one or two aspects, such as school variables and/or family circumstances and/or special educational needs (Parsons *et al.* 1994; Hayden 1997). Recent conferences have attempted to pull the different areas together, but research designs have tended to concentrate on inspection of one or two comparable variables rather than consideration of the all-embracing and inter-relating systems within which the child functions. The present study is the first to bring together the three systems of the child, the family and the school, and, in addition, includes comparisons with a matched group of non-excluded pupils.

Overview of the study

We decided to recruit a group of 20 excluded pupils, from within a single LEA in Greater London which had agreed to host the research project. Initial contact with parents of excluded pupils was achieved by the LEA sending a letter to all parents of pupils who became permanently excluded from school during the 12-month period (1996–7) we had set aside for data collection. This letter explained that an independent study into exclusions from school was currently taking place in the borough, and that they and their child might be contacted to find out if they were willing to take part in this. The LEA also informed us of each new permanent exclusion, and we then wrote to the parents (enclosing an appropriately worded letter for them to pass on to their child, if they themselves were ready to take part in the research) outlining the research project. We emphasised that, although participation would not alter anything to do with the child's exclusion, it would give parents and child the opportunity to share their thoughts and feelings at a stressful and worrying period in all their lives. Parents who wished to take part were asked to return a prepared card in a prepared stamped addressed envelope.

It proved remarkably easy to reach our target of 20 excluded pupils. Of the first 23 parents we contacted in this way, 20 agreed to take part. This willingness to participate seems to us to indicate a desire on the part of these families to 'tell their story' to someone they saw as being interested in their child's current situation and experiences. It was markedly more difficult to recruit the group of 20 non-excluded pupils who would act as the comparison group. For each excluded child, we needed to recruit a child of the same age, gender and ethnicity and attending the same school, who had never been either temporarily or permanently excluded from any school, and who was considered an unlikely candidate for exclusion of any kind in the future. We asked the school attended by each excluded child to select from the school register children who met the above criteria, and we then approached the parents of the first pupil on the register so identified. This was also done by letter in the first instance (again enclosing an appropriately worded letter for them to pass on to their child, if they themselves were ready to take part in the research), outlining the research study and saying we now wanted to meet with children who had never been excluded from school, and their parents. Parents who were willing to take part were again asked to return a prepared card in a prepared stamped addressed envelope. We had to approach a total of 34 families in this way before we reached our target of 20 matched comparison children.

The sample of excluded pupils we recruited in this way was

essentially an opportunity sample, yet we have some data to suggest that it is likely adequately to represent the overall population of excluded pupils. Of our 20 pupils 19 were excluded from secondary schools (95 per cent of the sample, cf. 81 per cent of the population of excluded pupils). Of our sample 15 had been excluded while they were in Years 9 or 10, the most common years for exclusions to occur in the excluded population. Black African-Caribbean pupils were over-represented in our sample: these pupils comprise 5 per cent of the LEA school population but they made up 10 per cent of our sample. The ratio of boys to girls in our sample was 4:1, exactly mirroring the current steady ratio in the population of excluded pupils. We are therefore reasonably confident that our results can generalise beyond the boundaries of the LEA in which the study was situated.

As already stated, our study was designed to investigate the ways in which complex interrelations between aspects of the children themselves, and of their families and schools, had combined to result in the child being permanently excluded from school. In Chapter 2, we set out the underlying theoretical bases of our enquiry, with a discussion of systems theory and narrative theory. In Chapter 3, we describe the characteristics of the children we chose to investigate, explain the theoretical rationale behind these choices, and present data showing the ways in which children in the excluded group were similar to and different from those in the comparison group. In Chapter 4, we turn our attention to the families in which the children were living. We present evidence from previous research of the kinds of family stressor that can impact adversely on children's development, and of the ways families have of coping with such stressors that can differentially affect the outcomes for children. We then describe the stressors and resilience to stressors revealed in our interviews with parents and children, and show how these were again similar in some ways across families of children in the excluded and comparison groups, and markedly different in others. Chapter 5 looks at the schools from which the children had been excluded. We use literature from previous research to introduce some of the factors that serve to define the ethos of a school, and the ways in which schools can differ along various dimensions, and how these things can affect pupil outcomes. This is illustrated by comparisons of high and low excluding schools in our sample. In Chapter 6, we move from considering the children as a group, to a more detailed consideration of four individual cases. In this chapter, we try to show

how the three systems of child, family and school interact and occasionally collide to produce exclusion. The final chapter of our book relates our findings back to the overall theoretical perspectives of systems and narrative theory, and attempts to map out some useful ways forward towards reducing permanent exclusions from school.

Chapter 2

Ways of understanding complexity

Systems and narrative theory

Children grow up within a network of complex systems. These include the child's own inner world (a system comprising, for example, personality, attribution, innate abilities), the family (a system comprising, for example, culture, dynamics between family members, family structures, family scripts) and school (a system comprising, for example, culture and ethos).

The research described in this book is concerned with collecting data relating to characteristics within these three interrelating systems, working with a group of permanently excluded pupils and their families, and a matched comparison group. The aim of the research was to present a coherent picture of which children, under what circumstances, are likely to be excluded from school, and which parts of which systems need to address change, in order to 'reduce serious stress, failure and unhappiness in children to enable them to grow up to be secure and confident people, able to fulfil their educational potential, play their part in society and be good enough parents to the next generation' (Enfield 1997: 1).

Research carried out within a systemic framework is concerned with the concept of organised complexity. One way of managing complexity is to reduce it, by examining parts of the system. This reductionist model will work perfectly well for mechanical systems: for example, if a car gearbox is faulty, it can be isolated, fixed and put back into the car engine systems, with no effect upon the other functioning systems of the car. However, a reductionist model is not effective in addressing the complexities of human relationships, where tinkering with any one aspect of a system of interconnected relationships will inevitably impact upon, and change, the whole system. Tempting as it might be in its apparent simplicity, it is not feasible to reduce the complexities when applying a systems framework in social science: reducing them in one's mind does not mean that they don't continue to exist. A more appropriate and meaningful approach is to find ways of understanding the complexities rather than reducing them.

In this chapter we will consider some of the important developments in systems thinking which have emerged in response to the challenge of understanding interrelating human systems in all their complexity. We will illustrate important concepts with reference to the three systems of child, family and school.

What is a system?

A system can be defined as a set of interrelated elements, each of which is related directly or indirectly to every other element, and no subset of which is unrelated to any other subset (Ackoff and Emery 1972). Although human behaviour is studied by a range of different professionals, including psychologists, anthropologists, psychiatrists and sociologists, the application of systems theory has developed particularly within the fields of psychology and psychopathology (Capra 1982).

Subsystems and boundaries

Systems divide hierarchically into subsystems, which in turn divide into further subsystems, and so on. A system at one level can be redefined as a subsystem at another level. For example, as shown in Figure 2.1 in the case of a child, the child's family can be seen as the

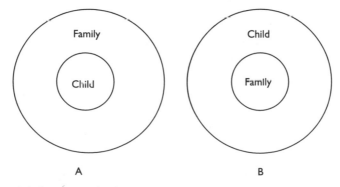

Family

Child

A

Child

Family

B

Figure 2.1 Systems and subsystems

system (A), or it can be seen as a subsystem of the child's inner world (B).

A boundary is therefore required between the system and the environment. Boundaries delineate the components which belong to the system and those which belong to the environment. Hall and Fagan (1956) define the environment as the 'place' where the system behaves – 'a set of objects a change in whose attributes affects the system' – and acknowledge that changes within the system likewise affect the environment.

Open and closed systems

Pertinent to the study of social systems is von Bertalauff's (1950) idea of 'open' and 'closed' systems. Reed and Palmer (1972) describe an open system as one which depends for its survival and growth upon an exchange of energy, materials, people and information with its environment. Both an individual and a school can be an open system, with each having both an internal and an external world, with a boundary between the two, across which the environment is regulated.

A 'closed' system is one which sets up barriers with its external environment. During the course of our long involvement in education we have seen schools move from closed systems where, in their most extreme and concrete, there was a line painted in the school playground over which parents were not allowed to cross, to open systems where parents are welcomed into schools and actively encouraged to participate in school life. Openness implies an ability to change within the environment and maintain a continual and steady state or 'equilibrium' (Cannon 1938).

Maintaining the equilibrium of a system

The concept of equilibrium might be best illustrated by considering the conflicting demands which are currently being made upon schools to enable all their pupils to achieve externally determined academic targets, whilst simultaneously requiring them to meet the educational needs of children from a wide range of abilities and circumstances. In the face of these seemingly incompatible demands, many schools are at present struggling to reorganise themselves to achieve a state of equilibrium. A related idea is that despite human interactions being dynamic and in a constant state of flux, there is a tendency for them to preserve a homeostatic balance in the face of changing circumstances. This can take the form of resistance to change.

Gillham (1981) and Dowling and Osborne (1994) refer to the maintenance of disruptive behaviour in some individuals as contributing to the maintenance of the status quo of an institution which might otherwise be challenged. Families and schools can collude successfully to maintain equilibrium at the expense of the 'symptomatic child'. In the school context, Gillham asks what it is in the school situation that is helping to maintain the behaviour. This question can be asked of all the subsystems involved in the present study – the child, the family and the school, as well as of the whole which is made up of these three interrelating parts.

The family and the school as systems

The study of the family as a system can be conceptualised as the investigation of a series of relationships between the interrelated systems of the individual, the family subsystems, the family system, and the family's environment. The individual family member is conceptualised as an organised system living within multiple systems, each, whether large or small, with biological, psychological and social characteristics.

In the same way, such a conceptualisation and theoretical framework can be adopted in the study of the child's school. Like families, schools consist of patterned activities of individuals, each complementary or interdependent, focused on common tasks and outcomes, and therefore a systemic framework can be seen as appropriate to the analysis of their function (Fisher 1986; Conoley 1987; Fish and Jain 1997). Like a family, a school has components of boundaries and subsystems. The challenge for the school system is to find ways to integrate the fragmented experiences of its members (teachers, pupils, non-teaching staff) into a meaningful whole. The starting point towards such integration is for a school to acknowledge that all its processes, procedures and activities make up the whole, and that each component affects and is affected by all of the other components.

The recipe for the successful functioning of a family and the successful functioning of a school system can be described similarly in terms of clarity of boundaries, and communication and cohesiveness within and between the subsystems.

Circular causality and the avoidance of blame

One of the sources of complexity in human systems is the fact that human interactions are driven by communication (Bateson 1958), which is usually multifaceted, and takes place at a number of verbal and non-verbal levels. Patterns of interaction and communication tend to recur over time, and may also be sustained through feedback. A child who gains adult attention through misbehaviour is often using the misbehaviour as a way of getting the attention, although not necessarily in a conscious way. Through a different feedback (such as ignoring the misbehaviour and giving attention to appropriate behaviour) the attention-seeking child is likely to employ different (more acceptable) behaviours to gain attention. These interacting patterns tend to be circular rather than linear, and give rise to circular, rather than linear, explanations. Circular explanations emphasise that causes reside in the interactional processes between two or more people, rather than solely in individuals.

Adoption of a circular rather than a linear approach to causality takes account of the interrelationships between an individual's systems, and moves away from a blame culture. As Dowling and Osborne (1994) emphasise, since the 1960s clinicians have moved towards placing individuals within the context of their families and systemic family therapy has developed as an alternative to treatment of individual pathology. Similarly, educationalists have moved away from solely within-child causes, to considering how pupils are affected by, for example, particular educational settings to which they belong. However, as Dowling and Osborne go on to say, the application of thinking systemically about schools has developed slowly and, in the main, separately from systemic work with families. This is unfortunate, as the two kinds of system do share common components and concepts. These include rules, punctuation, culture and belief systems, roles, and authority and power.

Rules

Gorell Barnes (1982) defines the ground rules of any system to be the specifics of the way a system functions. She defines the meta-rules as being about the meaning of the ground rules and reports that often the meta-rules attributed to a particular system reflect the wider context and may be a vehicle for the expression of the rules of other systems (e.g. society). This seems to be particularly pertinent at the present time with regard to school systems, where society is demanding 'evidence' of success in terms of academic results, through, for example, the publication of league tables.

Coulby and Harper (1985) state that it often takes a long time for someone to find out what the real school rules are. Often there are two sets of rules: one formal, which may be periodically written down and announced, and one which arises in an ad hoc way, or belongs to a specific teacher. One of the authors experienced insight into the application of school rules in one secondary school, not one used in our study, as described in the following story. The author, as the educational psychologist for the school, was invited by the senior management team to help them to think about what kinds of sanctions they should employ for those pupils who broke the school rules. The author agreed to the request, although being aware that before the staff could come to any agreement much thinking and sharing of their own views and values would be needed.

In a meeting with the whole senior pastoral team (comprising heads and deputy heads of year, the senior teacher and the deputy head teacher with responsibility for pastoral care and discipline) the author began by asking each member of the team to individually write down a list of the current school rules. Team members were then asked to share their list with another member of the team, and to report back to the whole group where there had been consensus and where there had been disagreement. The result was chaos. No team member had the same list as any other team member. Some longstanding staff members claimed that some rules, which more recently joined staff members had not listed as rules, had been in existence for many years. There followed a heated discussion between the team members about what were and were not school rules. The author eventually interrupted the discussion to ask simply, 'If the staff don't know the school rules, how can the pupils be expected to know them?' It was a salutary moment. It became clear to the team that pupils were being reprimanded by some staff but not by others for the same behaviours.

Similarly, in the family, there will be rules which may be explicit or implicit, and yet one parent may have his or her own idiosyncratic rules, thus mirroring the inconsistencies that exist outside the family. Most children are generally very good at discovering quickly what behaviour is required by different teachers and family members. However, a minority of children, and most probably those with some degree of learning difficulty, are less able to make such distinctions, and are, as a consequence, more often in trouble with particular teachers or with one parent.

Where schools have developed a positive school ethos, rules are in place to develop in the pupils qualities of self-discipline and co-operation, and not to demand blind obedience. The former is likely to be achieved where the rules are known, understood, discussed and endorsed, rather than where a long list of largely unnecessary restrictions is produced by teachers, and is unquestioningly enforced and expected to be unquestioningly obeyed. The implication is that in effective schools pupils have a powerful sense of their own self-worth and potential for achievement which is fostered by positive staff attitudes and behaviour. We see a clear link here to internal locus of control, which is one of the within-child variables assessed during our study.

Punctuation

Another systemic concept is that of 'punctuation'. Punctuation refers to the point at which a sequence of events is interrupted in order to give it a certain meaning; that is, what is deemed to cause what depends upon the way 'reality' is punctuated. The concept is illustrated in the following example, where we consider the importance of punctuation to analysis of events in school which can lead to pupils being punished or even eventually excluded. For example, in cases of bullying, a teacher who arrives on the scene at the point where the victim is stung into retaliation might wrongly assume that the victim is, in fact, the perpetrator. For such incidents the behaviourist approach of observing the *antecedence, behaviour and consequence* (ABC) of incidents can lead to a clearer understanding of cause and effect. However, even with such a systematic approach, the decision of where the antecedence occurs involves a punctuation of events. Punctuation is pertinent to the stories of the excluded pupils, their parents and the head teachers interviewed for our own study. The views and opinions presented depend upon the place where the different individuals punctuated incidents and experiences, as well as the time at which the interviews took place within the process of the exclusion – in the punctuation of events.

Culture, meaning and beliefs

An important emphasis of the application of systems theory relates to 'meanings', as a result of increasing recognition that the interactional field is not confined to people's behaviour, but includes systems of interconnected meanings. Meaning is seen as being held by individuals as their personal version of reality, and, as such, family difficulties can be seen as being caused by systems which hold problem-sustaining beliefs and meanings. This can also be applied to schools, where individual members hold personal versions of reality, which often serve to sustain their difficulties. Thus, a systemic approach involves a focus on interactive processes, including those that communicate meanings. It attempts to see these interactions in terms of patterns that may sustain problems.

Morgan (1986) describes culture as being a shared meaning, understanding and sense. She describes how, in a circular way, schools can reflect the parents' culture by developing attitudes which confirm the parents' perceptions of the school's ethos. For our study we investigated in some detail accounts of the school ethos of the schools which our excluded and comparison groups had attended. In relation to culture, Campbell (1988) describes meaning and behaviour as having a recursive or circular relationship, and proposes that we voluntarily behave as we do because we have certain beliefs about the context we are in, and that our beliefs are supported or challenged by the feedback from our behaviour.

Stoker (1992) warns that challenging belief systems can be dangerous. When he examined the strongly held belief by families, schools and education officials that children can be 'treated' and changed without any undue interference to their social system, his results indicated that to challenge such a belief is to challenge an entrenched power structure which will not readily change. Given the acknowledged powerful influences which schools and parents have on the formulation of children's development, including their internal attributions (for example, self-esteem and locus of control), it seems reasonable to assume that a greater understanding by those 'significant others' of the developmental processes involved could lead to changes in teaching and parenting styles, and school and family culture and belief systems.

Roles

One aim of the school can be seen as preparing pupils to work at the process of preparing to leave school sufficiently equipped to make a successful transition into adulthood. In order to do this, pupils must learn to interact with increasingly more diverse and complex systems. Pre-school children acquire, through the experience of being cared for within the family system, an idea of a bounded set of relationships. As children reach school age they enter even more complex systems and subsystems, thus needing to adapt their behaviour in response to change in the context and environment as they move from one system to another.

Taking up different roles is not as simple as learning a set of behaviours to be performed in a particular context. Where roles are prescribed there are few opportunities for individual expression. Where this is in the school environment, with children learning about who they are and developing their own beliefs and values, tension between internal needs and external demands is likely. In order to join new systems children need to work out new boundaries, new rules, new roles (of themselves and of others) and understand where the authority within the new system lies.

Bion (1961) proposes that behaviour operates at two simultaneous levels. At the work level, behaviour is directed towards the performance of a task and is the 'taking up a role' (acceptance of role) behaviour. The other level is what Bion refers to as the 'basic assumption level', which can be regarded as 'role avoidance' behaviour, or survival behaviour. This can be interpreted as a defence response to situations which feel threatening or unsafe. Bion describes four patterns of role avoidance behaviour as follows:

1   *Dependency*: this refers to the search for a more competent person to do the task or take over the role.
2   *Expectancy*: this refers to unrealistic expectations of outcomes which will occur as if by magic.
3   *Fight*: this refers to attempts to resist the task and the role.
4   *Flight*: this refers to a complete avoidance, a denial and giving up the task and the role.

In the case of children, these two simultaneous levels can be seen as developmental, with the 'basic assumption' level being more likely to be presented by immature or vulnerable children who are exposed to situations where they feel insecure, unfamiliar and unsafe. Many of the excluded pupils whom we met as a part of our study, and their teachers, demonstrated behaviours more consistent with avoidance, as described by Bion, than with his 'taking up the role' description. Examples of how each pattern of role avoidance can be observed within the pupil/school context are given below:

1   *Dependency*: Many teachers who had supported the exclusion of the pupils had done so in the belief that there was some other school or education provision that would be more competent to teach pupils with such challenging behaviour.

2   *Expectancy*: Teachers often believed that there existed some 'magic' formula, which, if the pupil and/or the parents were to follow, would make everything better. Excluded pupils often held a notion that if only a particular teacher were to behave in a different way, or leave the school, everything would be better. One of the authors recalls working with an 11-year-old boy (not involved in our study) who had been the victim and perpetrator of bullying in school, and had eventually attended a residential school for pupils with emotional and behavioural difficulties (EBD). This boy had significantly protruding teeth and told the author 'my life will be straightened out as soon as my teeth are straightened out'. There may well have been an element of truth in his statement insofar as much of the teasing and bullying to which he had been subjected had been in relation to his teeth, and his own bullying had been in response to how he himself had been treated. However, changing his physical appearance alone was unlikely to bring about the miracle result that he expected in his interpersonal relationships with other pupils.

3   *Fight*: Particularly where pupils found the task of learning difficult, there is much evidence from our research that they tended to take up a pattern of fight in relation to their learning. They acquired behaviours of resistance to their school work and environment, often adopting antisocial behaviours which were unacceptable to the school. Teachers also took on patterns of resistance where they experienced difficulties with pupils' challenging behaviours, often expressing the view that their role as teachers was to teach their subject, not to have to deal with unacceptable behaviour from some of their pupils. Fight is more evident in those schools where there exists a 'them and us' attitude within the pupil/teacher/parent community.

4   *Flight*: This is perhaps the most common pattern which we came across from both pupils and teachers in our study. The excluded pupils in our study who were experiencing difficulties, particularly in literacy skills, had often developed sophisticated strategies for completely avoiding the tasks, getting friends to complete work for them, 'losing' work (never having done it in the first place), volunteering to do tasks outside the classroom. Many admitted to being intentionally disruptive in class either to distract the teacher from the fact that they couldn't do the work given, or to get themselves sent out of the classroom, thus avoiding the work altogether. Teachers demonstrated patterns of flight by giving up attempts to work with challenging pupils, excluding them from the classroom and eventually from the school. Some teachers even decide to give up teaching altogether.

Where the structures and processes of systems (whether families or schools) are inconsistent and unclear, there is more likelihood of these survival behaviours being employed. Bion's work is clearly relevant to the enquiry in our own study into school ethos and family resilience, where clarity of roles and family routines are identified as protective factors.

Authority and power

Authority can be either legitimate or illegitimate. In order to accept and respond to authority appropriately, one needs to recognise its legitimacy or otherwise This will affect how one responds to authority, and recognises one's own authority. Authority is legitimate when it is within the context of an agreed role or task, but is illegitimate when based solely upon a person's status or personality; for example, when a teacher or parent justifies an instruction to a child by saying 'because I say so' or 'because that's the way it is'. Such illegitimate use of authority can be seen as arbitrary and idiosyncratic and can lead to feelings of unfairness and personal prejudice. Where authority is exercised legitimately it is likely to be experienced as consistent and supportive in ways which foster a sense of security and trust.

The notion of personal control can seem to be at odds with a systemic framework. In order to be totally in control of our lives we would need to be totally in control of the lives of those within our own and related systems. It is not difficult to recognise that this is impossible, and indeed undesirable. What is important within the model of circular causality is that when we feel sufficiently in control to change our own behaviour, we will inevitably recognise the part we play in changes in the behaviour of those around us. This will happen whether the behaviours are positive or negative, and it is the interrelationship between cause and effect which some institutions find difficult to appreciate, believing that only one part of the system needs to change. What affects children will inevitably affect their schools and their families.

Narrative theory

For our study we collected a great deal of information from listening to the stories of the experiences of the pupils, parents and teachers. We were not concerned with trying to establish what was real and true, but concerned only about individuals' own recollections of what they had experienced. Reissman (1993: 64) emphasises that 'the historical truth is not the primary issue. Narrativization is a point of view'. This way of eliciting information comes within the realm of narrative theory.

Narrative theory began at the start of the twentieth century as a science of narrative form and structure. Over the last 20 years, however, it has been transformed and expanded, mainly through incorporating postmodern ideas (Currie 1998). Although narrative theory is now applied to a highly diverse range of fields such as historical and literary criticism, its relevance to therapeutic work lies in its view that humans are narrative animals and the tellers and interpreters of their stories or narratives.

In this context, narrative theory proposes that our personal reality is organised and maintained through the construction of multiple stories about ourselves and those we relate to; that life is a matter of telling ourselves stories. In other words, we live through stories. Stories are not *about* life, they *are* life as we experience it. They are the way we make sense of events by placing them into meaningful sequences over time (Friedman and Combs 1996; Dallos 1997). These stories or narratives have a number of important characteristics. The structuring of narratives is thought to be a highly selective process. In describing this process, White (1995) emphasises that a lot of lived experience goes unstoried, remaining amorphous and without organisation or shape. This unstoried experience can include feelings, thoughts and actions, and can relate to the past, the present and even the future (White and Epston 1990). Burr (1995) makes a related but slightly different point that the sense of self and of the world are inevitably fragmented, having a multiplicity of potential versions, each the product of social encounters and relationships which are not necessarily consistent with each other.

Narratives give rise to meaning. Selected experiences are constructed as stories and these constructions give rise to a set of interpretations or meanings about the self, and about relations with others. These interpretations or meanings then determine behaviour. Narratives are dynamic and ever-renewing. This renewal process occurs with each interaction in which the individual is involved with the outside world. In this way people are seen as continually and actively re-authoring their lives from moment to moment, the self continually recreating itself through narratives which include other people who are reciprocally woven into these narratives (Friedman and Combs 1996).

Narratives are primarily laid down in language. The narrative or story metaphor is essentially one of language, both oral and written. White is quite clear, however, that non-language aspects of experience are incorporated within the concept of narrative, particularly feelings and intentions (White and Epston 1990). All narratives are not equal. Some narratives are more dominant than others. Where the dominant narratives are problem saturated, these may eclipse more enabling narratives (White and Epston 1990).

Is narrative theory compatible with systems theory?

The rationale for focusing on stories and the meanings that arise from them lies in the assumption that people's personal stories about themselves and others act as an organising framework for their behaviour in all life situations, including those within the family. The focus on life stories is one of the reasons why family therapists have shown an increasing tendency over the past decade to work with individuals (Tomm 1998). Minuchin (1998) argues that narrativists have lost the systemic approach since typically they interact with each member of the family in turn as individuals, and no longer focus on interactional patterns of behaviour. He claims that they focus on the individual rather than on social relatedness, and have become preoccupied with the power of cultural discourses at the expense of family process. One of the questions addressed in subsequent debates has been that of how one-to-one work stands up to the systemic microscope. In these circumstances, therapist and patient are working in the interactional space between them to identify new narratives. The problem-determined system of meanings within existing stories is likely to be maintained by interactions with significant others (alive or dead) which serve to sustain the problem. The systemic approach would require a focus on that interactional world. In individual therapy this can be achieved through working with the patient's internalised voices of significant others (Tomm 1998), thus having a focus that is described by Anderson (1999) as not the person, but the person-in-relationship.

Exploring the perspective of these inner voices and how in verbal or non-verbal ways they communicate and feed back to the individual's core self is arguably a systemic way of working. However, in contrast with Minuchin's approach, the therapist is interacting not with the family out there, but with an internalised version of that family within one individual. Not all narrativists who work with individuals stress the use of internalised voices, including White (1995), who emphasises the appropriateness of other techniques which are not in themselves systemic, such as 'identifying unique outcomes'. Arguably therefore, among narrativists who work with individuals, some do so in a more systemic way than others, particularly those who make active use of working with the idea of internalised voices.

Sluzki (1998) defends the incorporation of narrative into the systemic approach, and refers to 'narrative based systemic practices'. Friedman and Combs (1996) also defend the technique of exploring the narratives held by individuals in turn, by stressing that this is a relational experience with all present bearing witness to what is said. They also stress that the meaning making involved in narrative work is a radically interactive activity. Even though family interactions are not the direct focus of attention, as Minuchin would require, the beliefs that drive these interactions certainly are, and narrativists particularly focus on those beliefs that are incorporated from the cultural context in which the family lives (Schwartz 1999). Tomm (1998) stresses the fundamental importance of family members (or equivalent) in the generation and maintenance of specific meanings within narratives.

Narrativists also stress that new narratives will create a different system of meanings for the family, which may then be influenced by feedback loops in much the same way as in the classical Milan approach exemplified by Minuchin, where the system of beliefs sustaining the problem is also central. Indeed, one of the main similarities between the Milan approach and narrative work is that both privilege systems of meanings that sustain problems. The differences between the two approaches relate more to the level of meanings that are focused upon, and to the techniques used to bring about helpful change.

Thus, narrativists see the development of personal stories, including problem-sustaining stories, as an interactional process. The family (or equivalent) is held to have an important role in this, especially through the way it plays out wider cultural discourses such as gender roles. In bringing out new and previously marginalised stories, interactional techniques are used. It is clear therefore that narrativists rely on systemic theory in the way they interactionally work with meanings, and in the way they create circumstances whereby interactions in the meaning systems of the family can occur. Their work with families is therefore consistent with systemic ideas, even though their techniques, which do not focus on interactions within the session, are clearly different from those of Minuchin.

In our own study, narrative theory is applied in the use of semi-structured interviews which were used to elicit the stories, or narratives, of the participants. The study therefore is not concerning itself with the 'truth' or with the facts, but with the perceptions and memories of the participants, and comparing the differences in the accounts which each gives of the same incident and event. This is particularly shown in Chapter 6 where the stories of some of the exclusions are presented by the pupils, parent(s) and head teachers involved in each. Narrative theory is also applied in the descriptions that the parents and pupils give of family events and histories. Individuals do present different narratives about the same event, using facts and interpretations to shape new facts and new interpretations.

Chapter 3

Understanding the children

Ability, attainment, self-esteem and locus of control

In this chapter, we examine factors within the children themselves that might have contributed to their difficulties in school. Throughout this discussion, we bear in mind that these factors in themselves are heavily influenced by the children's genetic, social and developmental histories. Children become who they are through complex interactions between the innate qualities with which they are born and the structure of and relationships within the families in which they are raised, as well as by the ways in which these family structures and relationships interact with and are influenced by the wider society, including school.

Common sense suggests that children who do not do well at school will be more likely to become disaffected pupils who will find avoidance strategies, sometimes unacceptable, which put them at risk of exclusion. There are many aspects of school life that can lead (usually unintentionally) to pupils being emotionally hurt, embarrassed and humiliated. Pupils are expected to do well and to meet set targets. They are in competition against agreed set criteria and against each other. Public identification of the less able student can lead to humiliation, and the school context can provide a constant reminder of inadequacy. Even the most stimulating, creative and accommodating schools cannot always be so, and children who find the work difficult and who are not motivated to take the long term view that working hard at difficult tasks can lead to success, and eventually to enjoyable and worthwhile jobs, can easily lose interest. Whereas the majority of pupils may tolerate a degree of boredom in school, and acknowledge a system in which they have a task (as pupils) to complete, the pupil who experiences a sense of academic failure may be unable to tolerate the boredom and become disruptive and challenging.

Cognitive ability in relation to exclusion

There is some research evidence that supports the common-sense view outlined above. Parsons (1999: 47) reports that a significant number of permanently excluded pupils have struggled with school-work prior to their exclusion, concluding that 'there has been inadequate attention to individual learning needs'. Blyth and Milner (1996) describe the tensions that may be experienced in school by pupils unable to meet the demands of the schoolwork set or keep up with the rest of the class. They present quotations from young adults who remembered feelings of stupidity, frustration and anger at not being able to keep up and understand the work. These pupils had felt excluded from the whole activity of learning and in many cases their frustration found an outlet in challenging behaviour. Blyth and Milner also pick up on the point that feelings of being 'different' provided a 'powerful weapon' for children to use against each other, with the victims of early teasing or bullying quickly learning ways of defending themselves against this by being proactive and becoming the teasers and bullies themselves.

Cullingford (1999) reports that young offenders (many of whom had been excluded from school) who did not achieve academically felt that they only received attention when they did poorly with their work. However, once this additional attention was provided, it became more obvious to their peers that they were struggling and needed extra help. This is an example of a circular causality, where a pupil receives insufficient help and therefore does poorly, so receives additional help to address poor performance, and thereby becomes easily identifiable by peers as having difficulties and thus becomes humiliated and embarrassed. Young offenders reporting this dilemma appreciated the additional help provided by their teachers, but acknowledged that there was a price to pay for it.

Hayden (1997) reported that over a third of the case study children in her work with primary school exclusions had a Statement of Educational Needs at the time of their exclusion. Another third had a statement by the time they were interviewed for Hayden's study. Of these, 14 were identified as having emotional and behavioural difficulties (EBD) and three had EBD and moderate learning difficulties (MLD). Only one pupil had a Statement solely on the basis of learning difficulties. Hayden points out that, ironic-ally, after his exclusion from school, this pupil was transferred to an EBD special unit.

It is difficult to determine whether the frustrations that result from learning difficulties lead some children to present behaviour difficulties, or whether it is the presence of challenging behaviour that is not conducive to learning or to academic progress. It is likely to be a combination of the two explanations, leading to the development of a vicious circle which results in greater difficulties in both learning and behaviour. A linear view of causality cannot encompass the complexities of the relationships between learning and behavioural difficulties.

In the light of the associations reported above between poor academic performance and exclusion from school, we felt it important to assess the cognitive abilities of the children in our sample, and so each child was given a full IQ assessment, using the Wechsler Intelligence Scale for Children. Mean full scale IQ for children in the excluded group was 85.2 (standard deviation, henceforward sd, 11.9) whereas that of the children in the comparison group was 99.7 (sd 13.2). Thus, the comparison group mean was close to the population mean, whereas the excluded group mean was 1 sd below the population mean. This difference was statistically significant when examined using one-way analysis of variance (f, 1; 38 df = 13.20, p < .001).

Importantly, the excluded children performed worse on the verbal than the non-verbal scales (mean verbal IQ = 84.5, sd 11.4; mean performance IQ = 90.0, sd 14.4). Investigation of performance on the subtests of the verbal scale showed that the excluded group scored significantly lower than the comparison group on two of the verbal subtests, vocabulary (excluded mean, 7.0, sd 2.53; control mean 9.05) and comprehension (excluded mean, 6.50, sd 2.16; control mean 9.70).

These results do have important implications for teachers: children in the excluded group were more likely to experience difficulties with their expressive and receptive language. Such difficulties can affect pupils' ability to comprehend and follow verbal instructions both in and out of school, and are also likely to affect their ability to express themselves articulately in a social context. Where young people are *expected* to understand language – where no recognition of any difficulty exists – any inappropriate behaviour, response or reaction is likely to be interpreted as non-compliance and disobedience rather than misunderstanding or frustration. For example, one of the excluded pupils who had demonstrated weak verbal skills described one teacher as saying to him 'Don't you understand plain English?' on an occasion when he remembered being unclear what the teacher had been telling him to do. He reported that he had felt stupid and embarrassed in front of his friends and had eventually told this teacher to 'fuck off'.

In fact, several children in the excluded group reported not always being clear about what teachers were asking them to do, and being surprised by teachers getting angry with them. There was also some evidence from the pupil interviews that some of the excluded group were unable to cope with the subtleties of verbal teasing or sarcasm whether this was used by teachers or by other pupils. The following conversation between 'Peter' and a science teacher illustrates this:

Peter: So he said 'what's your game boy?' and I said that I didn't have a 'Game Boy' and he said 'Your game boy, what's your game then?' and I said I wasn't playing a game and he said I was winding him up and the other kids were laughing and he said something like let's all play games and I didn't know what he was going on about and I think he was just a bit round the twist.

Peter said that this incident led to him being sent outside the classroom and another teacher had come along and he got into more trouble. He described still not understanding what he had done wrong.

With much of education in schools being delivered verbally, pupils with poor language comprehension skills are likely to be disadvantaged and unlikely to follow whole lessons, or even activities outside the classroom such as school assembly. Although, as will be shown later, most of the excluded pupils were excluded for actions which took place outside the classroom environment, pupils reported frustration in class as possibly making them more likely to 'let rip' at break times. When they did get into trouble, most pupils said that they were usually sent to a senior member of staff and told to say what they had done. They reported that they often had to do this with other teachers and/or other pupils listening. Where these pupils had difficulties in expressing themselves verbally and in articulating their thoughts and ideas, such an exercise often led to the pupil feeling frustrated and humiliated. Indeed the excluded pupils used words such as 'hacked off' and 'pissed off' to describe their feelings of frustration and 'I felt a right dick-head' and 'She made me feel like a right prick' to describe feelings of humiliation. Such language, when used in school to teachers, particularly in front of their colleagues or other children, is understandably considered to be unacceptable and seen as further evidence of a pupil's insolent behaviour.

Literacy skills in relation to exclusion

Again common sense suggests that poor literacy skills might make it difficult for pupils to keep up in school. There is much research evidence suggesting an association between reading difficulties and behavioural difficulties in school (e.g. Rutter 1975; Frick et al. 1991; Hinshaw 1992). The causal direction of this relationship is still debated, with some authors (e.g. Leach and Raybold 1977; Stott 1981; Carlisle 1983; Williams and McGee 1994) suggesting low reading performance can create a 'poor get poorer' pattern of linguistic disadvantage. They suggest that this downward spiralling leads to despondency and a rise in behaviour difficulties. However, other authors (e.g. Rutter and Yule 1970) suggest that behavioural problems interfere with learning and hence give rise to reading difficulties. Again, it would seem that a linear view of causality is insufficient to explain the levels of complexity among these relationships. What seems clear is that inability to read to the level required to access information from set texts prevents a pupil from starting, let alone completing, tasks set in school, and leaves the pupil feeling disconnected and excluded from the whole learning experience.

We therefore felt it important to assess each child's literacy skills, and used three subtests of the Wechsler Objective Reading Dimensions (WORD) to this purpose, from which we gained age equivalents for word reading accuracy, text comprehension and spelling. The comparison group achieved significantly higher age equivalents than the excluded group on all three measures (word reading accuracy, comparison group mean age = 13.35, sd = 2.80; excluded group mean age = 10.72, sd = 3.7; $f(1,38df) = 5.87$, $p < .03$; text comprehension, comparison mean age = 13.24, sd 2.3; excluded mean age = 10.25, sd 3.3; $f(1, 38$ df$) = 10.17$, $p < .01$; spelling, comparison mean age = 12.68, sd 3.2; excluded mean age = 10.01, sd 3.1; $f(1, 38$ df$) = 7.19$, $p < .01$). Bearing in mind the distribution of chronological age within each group, with 15 children in each group aged between 13 and 15, it is clear that many of the excluded children had reading and spelling ages well below their chronological age, whilst most of those in the comparison group were reading (but perhaps not spelling) at an age-appropriate level.

Where pupils experience literacy difficulties they are seriously disadvantaged across most of the school curriculum. It is likely therefore that poor literacy skills contributed to the disaffection of the excluded pupils which led ultimately to their permanent exclusion from school. Some of the pupils acknowledged to us that they were embarrassed to ask for help with their reading, and that they preferred to avoid all work that required them to read or write. This often meant that they seldom produced homework and would get into trouble for presenting either too little or no work at all in the classroom. They reported that they preferred to get into trouble for 'messing around' than to be thought of, by teachers and peers, as being 'thick'. An example of this is shown in the following extract from our interview with Kevin:

> I can't be bothered to try to read stuff what I know I can't – what's the point? It always takes me ages and I can do it but it takes me longer and everyone else just does it so I can't be bothered so I end up messing about you know flicking paper and that and then the teacher sends me out so I don't have to do the work then . . . then I've got nothing written for the next time we have history. If the other kids knew I can't read very good they'll think I'm thick and I'll be like those thickos.

The powerful experience and fear described by those pupils who did have reading difficulties of being seen, particularly by their peers, as 'thick' seems to result in an overwhelming need to hide their difficulties. Some of the pupils said that it had been easier to ask for help when they were at their primary schools but once they started secondary school it was too difficult. Some reported preferring to rely on help from their friends or parents rather than asking their teachers for help. Two of the excluded pupils told us that they covered up their poor spelling by making their writing difficult to read. They both said that they would then get told off for poor handwriting, which they saw as being preferable to being told off for poor spelling, which again they construed as being told that they were 'thick'. In contrast to the excluded group, those pupils in the comparison group who demonstrated weak literacy skills reported that, although they also used their friends and parents for help, they did ask their teachers for help and usually got it.

The results presented earlier for cognitive ability and literacy skills show that some excluded pupils demonstrated learning and/or literacy difficulties that would seem to warrant referral to an educational psychologist. Eight of the excluded group had cognitive ability scores more than one standard deviation below the norm, compared to only one of the comparison group. Eight of the excluded group had reading and/or spelling ages below 8.5 years, compared to only two of the comparison group. Of the six excluded children who had been referred to an educational psychologist before their exclusion, only two had been referred by their school. In 12 cases, the pupil's literacy difficulties were not mentioned in school records and had not been referred to by their school in reports of the exclusion, although in 8 of these cases mothers had expressed concerns about their child's poor reading. In contrast, the two comparison children referred to an educational psychologist had both been referred by their school. This might suggest that teachers have an implicit belief system that assumes reading difficulties are the consequence rather than the cause of bad behaviour, leading them to underestimate the need for intervention with apparently poorly motivated pupils. Alternatively, it might be that, conscious of the paucity of available resources, teachers prefer to refer on only those pupils whom they consider most likely to benefit from what is available.

Self-esteem

It is perhaps a truism among teachers that children who present behaviour difficulties in school have 'low self-esteem'. However, the concept of self-esteem is more complicated than this easy judgement might imply. In much of the educational literature, the terms 'self-esteem' and 'self-concept' are used interchangeably, whereas the psychological literature makes a clear distinction between the two. 'Self-concept' can be defined as the constellation of factual statements people use to describe themselves; for example, 'I am tall', or 'I am the only boy in my family'. 'Self-esteem' can be defined as an *evaluation* of the information contained in the self-concept, derived from people's feelings about all the things they think they are (Coopersmith 1967; Pope 1988).

The formation of self-esteem can be examined in terms of the 'perceived self' and the 'ideal self'. The perceived self is the same as self-concept, a subjective view of skills, characteristics and qualities that are either present or absent. The ideal self is the image of the person one would like to be, a sincere wish to possess certain qualities and characteristics. When the perceived self and the ideal self are a reasonably good match then self-esteem will be positive or 'high', but where there is a mismatch (I am not what I think I ought to be) the result will be negative or 'low' self-esteem.

Thus, it is the discrepancy between ideal and perceived self that leads to problems with self-esteem. People with 'high' self-esteem will hold realistic beliefs of their strengths and weaknesses, and will not be too harshly critical of the latter. People with 'low' self-esteem may exhibit an artificially positive self to the world, in what might be an attempt to prove to others, and to themselves, that they are 'adequate', whilst actually not quite believing it themselves. Alternatively they may retreat, fearing that contact with others will bring about rejection and alienation because of assumed inadequacies. According to both Coopersmith (1967) and Pope (1988), levels of self-esteem are relatively stable across momentary situation-driven shifts in self-evaluation.

Family influences on the development of self-esteem

When considering the relationship between levels of self-esteem and exclusion, it is important to understand the antecedents of this relatively stable construct. There is much evidence that children develop positive or negative self-esteem mainly according to what they learn about themselves from significant others (e.g. parents, teachers). Thus, when addressing the internal attributions of self-esteem it is necessary, in a systemic framework, to consider these characteristics in the context of the wider systems of the child's world, specifically the family and the school. The long-term developmental influences that lead to formation of a relatively stable level of self-esteem are probably more important factors in school exclusion than the four concurrent sources of self-esteem identified by Coopersmith:

- 'power' (i.e. the ability to influence and control others)
- 'significance' (i.e. the acceptance, attention and affection of significant others)
- 'worthiness' (i.e. adherence to moral and ethical standards)
- 'competence' (i.e. successful performance in meeting demands for achievement).

Children who get excluded from school are unlikely to feel either powerful or competent, and these feelings could follow from the experience of exclusion. However, they might still be high achievers in other aspects of their life, unknown or unvalued by the school (such as knowledge of pop music or football teams), thereby allowing for preservation for self-esteem through feelings of significance. It is by living up to aspirations in areas which children regard as being personally significant that they maintain high self-esteem.

The psychoanalytic view of development of self-esteem

In terms of the long-term development of self-esteem, psychoanalytic practitioners such as Miller *et al.* (1993) hold the view that from the earliest interactions with the mother, the infant is processing positive feelings of warmth, security, value and a sense of being 'known'. These are the experiences that, from the very beginning, provide the foundations for positive self-esteem. Alternatively, the newborn baby may experience negative feelings of coldness, rejection, emotional absence, and experiences which may provide unstable and rocky foundations for the development of self-esteem. Miller *et al.* promote the importance of the very beginnings of the mother–infant relationship, of the powerful experience of being loved and 'known' for themselves, where the mother is 'taken in' by the child, and where each feels loved from the 'inside' – the feelings of unconditional positive regard. Miller *et al.* explain that children who have 'good enough' self-esteem will not be overwhelmed by their 'bad' feelings, and do not begin to suppose that they have to be perfect children, either always good, or always clinging, helpless nonentities in order to protect themselves from their 'awful wickedness'. When consistency is weak the only way to protect the cherished parts of the self from the unwanted parts is to split them apart. When the 'good' and the 'bad' are split, the wholeness of the self fragments and disintegrates, and it then becomes impossible to appreciate and respect the wholeness of others. It is important for individuals to be able to define an event filled with negative implications and consequences in a way that does not detract from their general sense of worthiness, ability and influence.

A study by Ricks (1985) lends some support to the psychoanalytic view. He found that mothers of securely attached children had higher self-esteem and reported more positive recollections of childhood relationships with their own mothers, fathers and peers, than those who had insecurely attached infants. Especially important were mothers' recollections of having been accepted by their own mothers during childhood, which was also significantly linked to self-esteem. This developmental pathway describes children experiencing their own mothers' acceptance and subsequent development of high self-esteem, which helps them, in turn, to become competent parents to their own children.

The cognitive developmental approach to self-esteem

Developmental psychologists (e.g. Harter 1982) see the self-system as evolving and changing as children move from a largely physical sense of self in infancy to an appreciation of more abstract personal qualities as they grow through to adolescence. Harter therefore constructed self-esteem scales where different questions are posed according to the age of the child, and we considered these developmental scales most appropriate for use in our study. In the cognitive-developmental approach, families need to be both supportive and flexible, so that support can be adapted to suit the needs of children as these needs change over the course of childhood and adolescence. Fundamental conditions for the development of positive self-esteem identified by Coopersmith (1967) are:

- total or near total acceptance of children by their parents
- clearly defined and enforced limits
- respect for individual action that can exist within the defined limits.

His study clearly indicated that parents able to meet these three conditions are most likely themselves to have positive self-esteem. The correlation between positive self-esteem in parents and children indicates that unconscious identification and conscious modelling may well underlie the self-evaluations of individuals. However, parents with 'low' self-esteem who are accepting of their child may provide a negative model of esteem, yet at the same time, because at least one of the three necessary conditions is present, may lead their child to a higher level of self-appraisal than the parent has attained.

Baumrind (1967) proposed four key dimensions of child rearing patterns that can radically affect outcomes:

- the degree of warmth and nurturance parents express towards their children
- the extent to which parents expect children to be mature and independent
- the clarity of rules and consistency with which they are applied
- the amount and quality of two-way communication between parents and children.

From these key dimensions, Baumrind identified three styles of child rearing: permissive, authoritarian and authoritative. The permissive style is high in nurturance but low in maturity demands, control and communication. The authoritarian style is high in maturity demands and control, but low in nurturance and communication. The authoritative style is high in nurturance, control, maturity demands and communication (i.e. all four qualities). Bee (1989) proposes that, as a general rule, children who are raised by parents adopting an authoritative style tend to have 'high' self-esteem, and achieve 'earlier or more complete identity achievement in adolescence'.

Again, there is some evidence in support of these views. Halpin and Whiddon (1980) investigated perceived parental antecedents of self-esteem for Native American and white 12- to 18-year-old boys and girls. They found that instrumental companionship, nurturance, principled discipline and achievement reward were positively related to high self-esteem, while protectiveness, external punishment, achievement pressure, deprivation of privileges and affected punishment were negatively related. Rosenberg (1979) studied more than 5000 high school students and reported that adolescents who had closer relationships with their fathers were higher in self-esteem than were those who had more distant and impersonal relationships with their fathers. The study also highlighted that lone children, particularly lone male children, are higher in self-esteem than children with siblings, irrespective of birth order, and that social class is only weakly related to the development of self-esteem, with ethnic group affiliation being unrelated to self-esteem development.

School influences on the development of self-esteem

Unfortunately, much of the work on school influences discusses the development of self-concept rather than self-esteem. This in itself possibly indicates the confounding of these two distinct concepts in

much of the educational literature. We have found relatively few
studies that expressly investigate the influence of schools on the
development of children's self-esteem. Lawrence (1985) suggests that
friendly and supportive counselling by non-specialists in primary
schools can increase the self-esteem of children described as slow
readers. He claimed that long-term reading gains cannot reasonably
be expected without a corresponding change in the child's self-
esteem. Although the child may 'please the teacher' by learning skills
in the classroom, once away from the teacher the child with low self-
esteem is likely to perceive himself as a poor reader, unable to recognise or be encouraged by his improvement. In our own clinical work
one of us has frequently encountered children who, when asked 'Are
you a good, quite good, not very good or very poor reader?' answer
that they are 'very poor' in spite of scoring average or above average
on a standardised test of reading. This response can be baffling to a
teacher who may not have considered self-esteem to be an important
variable in the teaching and learning of reading.

It has also been shown (Leach and Raybold 1977) that children
with low self-esteem react differently to school failure and criticism
than children with high self-esteem. Those with low self-esteem were
more likely to react to school failure and criticism in more extreme
ways, showing withdrawal, aggression or both. Children with low
self-esteem tended to reflect their own general conclusion that they
were inadequate as people to meet the goal requirements of their
teachers. There is also some evidence that children with low self-
esteem are more likely to drop out of school. Reid (1982) conducted
a study into self-esteem of school drop-out students. His work found
that school drop-out students had fewer friendships with professional staff and were found to have lower self-esteem than non-drop-
out students. The implication from these findings is that students
who are disaffected are likely to have 'low' self-esteem. In the context
of our study, we should emphasise the difference between pupils who
drop out of school (i.e. those who choose not to attend) and pupils
who are excluded from school (told that they may not attend). The
excluded children in our study were, without exception, considered
to be good attenders.

Gurney's (1980) work showed secondary schools to have a debili-
tating effect upon the self-esteem of female pupils. Gurney suggests
that females need greater peer group acceptance during adolescence,
which leads to a demonstration of 'low' self-esteem. If this is the case
adolescent females will have lower estimations of themselves. There

is some evidence (Wolleat *et al.* 1980) that girls attribute success in school subjects to unstable factors such as an easy test on a day when they felt good, whilst males tend to attribute success in subjects to stable factors such as ability. This is consistent with the findings in the locus of control literature as will be shown later in this chapter. Wolleat *et al.* concluded that the self-esteem of females was significantly lower than that of males. No differences were found between the self-esteem of females from single-sex schools and co-educational schools. However, over all differences between school type and self-esteem for all pupils (male and female) was significant, largely due to a difference for boys. Thus school type seemed to have been more important for male self-esteem.

Self-esteem and exclusion from school

In previous work with excluded pupils (e.g. John 1996; Hayden 1997) low self-esteem has been shown to be associated with negative behaviour towards others, with exclusion serving to further damage the self-esteem. Hayden suggests that the manner in which the exclusion occurs increases the difficulties, so that stressed families become more stressed as a result of the exclusion and children with already low self-esteem suffer greater damage to their self-esteem. She also acknowledges that, in difficult and challenging circumstances, it may not be only the challenging child's self-esteem that is affected, but that the self-esteem of teachers and other children can be negatively affected too. John (1996) argues that low self-esteem goes some way to explain the difficulties of excluded pupils, saying that many young people with low self-esteem will often refuse to attempt work which they feel is beyond them and may justify their rejection by saying that it is 'crap' or 'boring'.

Results of our assessment of self-esteem

In the light of the literature reviewed above, we might expect to find that the excluded children in our study have lower self-esteem than the comparison children. To investigate this, we used the Harter scales for children (Harter 1982) and adolescents (Harter 1985). The scale for children is designed to assess the child's self-evaluation in six areas, with subscales for social acceptance, scholastic and athletic competence, physical appearance, behaviour conduct, and global self-worth. The scale for adolescents additionally assesses self-evaluation in respect of close friendship, romantic relationships and job competence. Both scales further assess the degree of support children feel they receive from their parents, their teacher and their class.

Global self-worth

Results for each subscale were analysed in Mann-Whitney tests that showed significant differences between the excluded and the comparison group in four of the subscales. Excluded children had significantly lower global self-worth: they liked themselves less as people, were less happy with the way they are leading their lives, and were generally less happy with the way they are. This supports the excluded pupils' school records and the two educational psychologists' reports that identified poor self-esteem.

Scholastic competence, behaviour and close friendships

The other three areas in which excluded pupils felt significantly worse about themselves were in their scholastic competence, their behaviour and close friendships. Given that the excluded group performed significantly worse than the comparison group on tests of cognitive and literacy abilities, their lower self-evaluations of scholastic competence might seem to reflect a realistic picture of their scholastic abilities, despite the fact that in six cases where the excluded pupils obtained IQ scores in the very low average range, their particular learning needs had not been identified by their teachers. In each case the educational needs were expressed by the school solely in terms of behaviour difficulties.

Similarly, since all had been excluded for unacceptable behaviour, they are perhaps giving a realistic appraisal of their own behaviour, coloured by their recent experience of exclusion. However, there is again some contradiction between this result and the way in which, during interviews, the excluded group described their behaviour as being no worse than that of other pupils who did not get excluded from school, and how they tended to blame other things or people for the fact that they got into trouble.

That they feel worse about their close friendships might also result from the experience of exclusion, which has likely disrupted any close friendships formed at school. In pupil interviews the excluded group talked about difficulties in maintaining contact with friends since their exclusion, and talked about feeling bored and isolated.

Athletic ability, physical appearance and romantic appeal

More interesting is the fact that in most of the areas investigated by the Harter subscales, the excluded children's levels of self-esteem were similar to those of the comparison group. Both groups felt equally confident about their athletic ability. From pupil interviews it was apparent that prowess in a sporting or physical activity, whether karate, football, snooker or disco dancing, was valued in both groups and seen as something which peers valued and admired. In the case of all three of the black African-Caribbean comparison pupils, sporting talent was reported by the pupil and by the parents. Although there was no significant difference in athletic self-esteem between the two groups, the interview data strongly suggested that the excluded group were less likely to have a particular interest or belong to a sporting club or team, even when the school described them as demonstrating a particular strength.

Both groups also felt equally confident about their physical appearance and had similar perceptions of their romantic appeal – their attractiveness to those to whom they are attracted, or are dating, or want to be dating, or want to feel that they are fun and interesting to be with on a date. However, it is interesting to note that, with one exception in the excluded group, none of the pupils had high romantic self-esteem. This might be most reasonably explained by noting the adolescent age range of the two groups, when most may be feeling uncomfortable with feelings of sex and romance.

Social acceptance

More unexpectedly, both groups evaluated themselves similarly with respect to social acceptance: the degree to which they felt accepted by peers, felt popular, felt they had friends and that they were easy to like. This was unexpected, given that exclusion from school is generally not seen as a good thing, either by adults or by other pupils. Data from the interviews that we present later when discussing the concept of locus of control may help to explain this unexpected finding. Every single excluded pupil saw exclusion from school as having many disadvantages, such as prevention of continuing education and difficulties in retaining friendships. However, if the pupils feel that the school exclusion was not their fault, they might also believe that those who matter most to them (their friends) will know and accept this and therefore they are able to continue to retain the social acceptance which they enjoyed prior to the exclusion.

What also is interesting is that the excluded pupils have been able to develop similar social acceptance self-esteem to the matched comparison group, given that there is an assumption that they have been presenting antisocial behaviour over a period of time, and that this should militate against their being socially accepted (at least at school). However, when we studied school records and data from pupil and parent interviews, for twelve (60 per cent) of the excluded pupils there was no record of long-term antisocial behaviour. The incidents that led to permanent exclusion were described in three cases as 'isolated but serious', in two cases as 'out of character', and in nine cases had developed over a relatively short period of time since the pupil had started at secondary school. In the remaining eight cases there was documented evidence of concerns about the pupils' behaviour over a period of time. In two cases parents described having worries when the pupil was at nursery school, and in six cases concerns were expressed by the primary school in Year 6 (the year before secondary transfer). These data therefore suggest that most of the pupils were producing acceptable social behaviours for most of their early development and that this had enabled them to develop positive social acceptance self-esteem.

Job self-esteem

The two groups were also similar in job self-esteem, in the extent to which they felt they had job skills and were ready to do well in part-time jobs. This is again surprising in the context of data from pupil interviews, where the excluded pupils expressed the view that their exclusion from school might disadvantage them when they try to find employment. It is obviously impossible to establish whether or not this group had more positive job self-esteem prior to their exclusion from school. As previously mentioned, situational self-esteem is relatively shortlived and self-esteem tends to be stable rather than situational. Given that these pupils were interviewed between three and six months after the exclusion it could be argued that the responses they gave in respect to this domain provide a stable measure. However this argument should be treated with caution, as 'exclusion from school' can be described as being a stable situation rather than 'situational', in that the situation continues and cannot be reversed. This is particularly pertinent in the case of those pupils (19 out of the 20) who did not get back into another school. For those pupils who were receiving no alternative education (N = 12) or who were attending short-term temporary education such as a pupil referral unit (N = 7) the 'situation' was still that of 'exclusion'; therefore 'situational self-esteem' might still apply.

Perceived support from parents, teachers, peers and friends

When we looked at data from the support scales, which assess the degree of support pupils feel they receive from parents, teachers, friends and their class group, excluded pupils did not differ from comparison pupils in the extent to which they felt supported by friends and the class. They did however feel significantly less well supported by both parents and teachers. Some of the excluded group reported their parents wanting to support them but feeling that they were incapable of doing so. In some cases this was seen as being because parents were unwell and incapacitated, and in some cases it was seen as being because parents did not know or understand the system, and/or did not speak English and so were unable to actively support their child. The assessment of parental support using the Harter assessment tool considered pupils' perception of general (non-specific) parental support and not, as in the case of the semi-structured interviews, exclusion specific perceptions. However, the excluded pupils were all aware that they were taking part in the study solely on the basis of having been permanently excluded from school. It is possible that they were focusing on the exclusion even when being asked questions relating to general situations. With regard to teacher support, in some cases the excluded pupils were able to identify teachers whom they did feel supported by, but described these teachers as not having sufficiently high status or power within the school as to be able to make a difference to the outcome of the exclusion.

Summary of self-esteem results

Overall, a rather complex picture of self-esteem emerges from these data, and one that is occasionally in conflict with data from pupil interviews. What seems clear is that it is in areas of the self most closely linked to school and the values espoused by school that the excluded children are most likely to feel badly about themselves. Some of these self-evaluations seem realistic: for example, low scholastic competence in the context of the children's measured scholastic skills. Others might be the result of the continuing situation of exclusion in which they find themselves: for example, negative evaluations of their behaviour and their close friendships. Some of the contradictions between the self-esteem measures and interview data will be discussed further when results from measurement of locus of control are considered.

Locus of control

The concept of locus of control is part of Rotter's (1954, 1966, 1982) Social Learning Theory of Personality and Attribution, and represents a generalised expectancy concerning the determinants of rewards and punishments in one's life. At one extreme are people with 'internal locus of control', who believe in their ability to control life's events; at the other extreme are people with 'external locus of control', who believe that life's events are the result of external factors which are beyond their control, such as luck and fate. The generalised expectancy of internal control refers to the perception of events, whether positive or negative, as being a consequence of one's own actions, and therefore under personal control. On the other hand, the generalised expectancy of external control refers to the perception of positive and negative events as being unrelated to one's own actions and behaviours, and therefore beyond personal control. In the context of the present study it is relevant to note that this can of course apply not only to children's own beliefs in their influence and control over what happens to them, but equally to how they will be affected and influenced by the beliefs of their parents and their teachers. The central tenet of Rotter's theory is that most learning occurs in interpersonal situations:

> It is a social learning theory because it stresses the fact that the major or basic modes of behaving are learned in social situations and are inextricably fused with needs, requiring for their satisfaction the mediation of other persons.
>
> Rotter (1954: 84)

Rotter's study and development of the concept of locus of control stemmed from considerations as to why some clients in psychotherapy appeared to gain from and change their behaviour as result of new experiences, whilst others seemed to discount new experiences. The latter group would attribute new experiences to chance, or to other people's actions, but not to their own behaviour or actions. The following case of Karl S is used by Phares (1976) to demonstrate this.

Karl S was seen by Phares for therapy for social-sexual and educational employment difficulties. It was the therapists' early hypothesis that Karl S's difficulties were due to his poor interpersonal skills. However, despite intensive didactic intervention, resulting in markedly improved interpersonal skills, Karl S continued to view his future negatively, and continued to be unable to relate any success to his own actions, but rather to ascribe success to good fortune:

> Therapeutic efforts were predicated on the assumption that as Karl S tried out various behaviours and witnessed their reinforcement, this would increase both his expectancy that those and similar behaviours would be successful in the future and his willingness to repeat them . . . This seemed to be the path of a 'tried and true' psychological principle.
>
> Phares (1976: 2)

The response of Karl S to reinforcement demonstrated to Phares and Rotter the inadequacy of learning theory. They began to recognise that Karl S considered reinforcement as being beyond his control, that his behaviour was not a major determinant in the receipt of rewards, and therefore considered that there was no point in expending energy in order to bring about success. Phares (1976) claimed that it was from this insight into Karl S's phenomenological world that the locus of control concept developed as an element of Rotter's social learning theory.

It follows from this theory that children will not learn from their experiences unless they believe that these experiences are actually related to their own actions. Rotter presented a considerable body of evidence that people learn differently in situations where rewards depend upon chance, luck, or the experimenter's whim, than they do in situations where they perceive that skill or their own characteristics determine whether or not a reward will occur. If individuals are subjected to a series of situations in which they have less control than other individuals, then the expectancies for lack of control that they develop become generalised to some degree. Consequently there may be significant and important individual differences in the degree to which people see their own lives as determined by their own behaviour and characteristics, or see their lives as controlled by luck, chance, fate or powerful others. It seems logical that the belief that one's own efforts can produce change is an important ingredient in getting people to better their lives, whether in the areas of adjustment, achievement, ecology, politics or social living.

Rotter (1982) warns that people are not totally 'internals' or 'externals', but will represent a distribution found in the normal population. The terms 'internal' and 'external' are used as expressive shortcuts and are not meant to imply that perception of control is a trait or typology. The perception of control is a process, the exercise of an expectancy regarding causation, with the terms 'internal' and 'external' depicting an individual's more common tendencies to expect events to be contingent or non-contingent upon their own actions.

Locus of control and attribution theory

Palenzuela (1984) recognised two areas of confusion in the locus of control concept: first, the distinction between 'locus of control' and 'causal attribution'; second, the place of 'locus of control' in the context of 'control'. The distinction between 'locus of control' and 'causal attribution' is by no means made in all the locus of control literature (Phares 1976; Lefcourt 1982). According to Zuroff (1990), the two concepts differ in that locus of control is evaluated prior to the outcome of an event (the perceived degree of control predicts the outcome) whereas attributions are made after the outcome of the event (with the benefit of hindsight, we determine the causes of the event).

Petterson (1987) made much the same distinction, arguing that there is a difference between people's perception of a given determinant as a cause of what happens to them (causal attribution) and their belief that they can control what happens to them (behavioural outcome contingency). In the first case, people identify the probable causes of an event, and classify each of these as internal or external in relationship to them. In the second case, however, once causality has been attributed to their own various personal characteristics or to the environment, people analyse the forces involved and sense whether they can influence the outcome in question through their own behaviour.

Weiner (1979) attempted to place locus of control within the wider attribution model, and describes two different dimensions. The first of these is the internal–external dimension, where a causal attribution is made either to factors within the person or within that person's environment. The second concerns the stability–instability of these causes. Later, he introduced a third dimension, that of 'controllability', whereby some internal unstable factors may be more controllable than others: for example 'effort' might be more controllable than 'mood'. Elliott (1993) exemplifies Weiner's model in relation to ability, as follows:

> Ability . . . could be considered as internal and stable, while mood would be internal, and, perhaps, unstable. Task difficulty could be considered external and stable, while luck would be external and unstable.
>
> (Elliott 1993: 111)

For example, children in school may consider that they have little or no 'control' over their ability, or over the learning task set by the teacher, but that they do have some control over other factors which will affect their success at the learning task, for example, who has upset them earlier in the day (mood), or whether or not their football team won on Saturday (luck).

The development of locus of control

For the purposes of our study, we were concerned only to *measure* locus of control, the degree of perceived control the pupils had over events in their own lives. But how does locus of control develop? There is agreement in the literature that as children grow older, they come to perceive themselves as more able to determine events around them (Lefcourt 1976) and there is thus overall a developmental trend towards internality (Nowicki and Strickland 1973). However, longitudinal studies have demonstrated more complex developmental changes. For example, Sherman (1984) found that, for some of the participants in his study, there was a strong swing towards externality at the age of 13 years. He proposed that this shift, coinciding as it did with the onset of puberty and related physical changes beyond the control of the individual, might indicate a relation between locus of control and cognition. This is particularly interesting within the context of school exclusion, given that exclusion from school is most common among 13 and 14 year olds. However, as the physical changes associated with puberty are occurring for all children at this age, it is also interesting that the shift towards greater externality did not occur for all the participants in Sherman's study. What is it that makes some adolescents resilient to this shift?

Locus of control, ethnicity and socio-economic status

Other studies suggest that there is a relationship between locus of control and ethnicity and socio-economic status. The literature which exists has struggled with separating ethnicity from socio-economic status. There have been mixed results from studies comparing locus of control in different ethnic groups, with Battle and Rotter (1963) and Rabinovitz (1978) claiming that black children are more external than white children, and Louden (1977) finding West Indian children living in the UK to be more external than English white or Asian children living in the UK. However these conclusions have been challenged by others (e.g. Banks 1991), and Remy (1983) found no differences between UK white, African-Caribbean and Trinidadian children. Dyal (1984) concluded, from a review of relevant studies, that socio-economic status is more significant than ethnicity in relation to locus of control. The review findings suggest that external locus of control is an appropriate reflection of the life conditions of less advantaged children and adolescents regardless of ethnicity. This conclusion implies a strong role for societal factors in the development of locus of control.

Locus of control, ability and academic achievement

Although Gammage (1985) found no relationship between IQ and internal locus of control, he considered that verbal intelligence does influence locus of control, thus highlighting a relationship between low verbal ability and external locus of control. Given that most communication that takes place between teacher and pupil is verbal communication, those pupils who have limited verbal ability (both receptive and expressive) are likely to experience poorer communication with their teachers than pupils with strong verbal skills.

There is a significant body of evidence associating internality with high academic achievement. Crandall et al. (1965) developed a scale for assessing children's beliefs that they, rather than other people, are responsible for their intellectual academic success and failures.

Normative data on 923 students in grades 3 to 12 indicated that self-responsibility was already established by grade 3, and that there were slight but significant differences in those subscale scores which were dependent upon the gender of the children, with older girls giving more self-responsible answers than older boys. Responsibility scores were moderately related to intelligence, ordinal position in the family, and inconsistently related to social class. Bar-Tar and Bar-Zohar (1977) reviewed 36 studies, 31 of which found a positive relationship between internality and academic achievement, with only one finding of a negative relationship between the two variables. Findley and Cooper (1983) reviewed 98 such studies and concluded that significantly more internal beliefs were associated with high achievement. Thompson (1990) also found a relationship between internality and higher levels of academic achievement in his study with a British population. Collier and Jacobson (1987) have suggested a relationship between internal locus of control and giftedness.

There are less conclusive findings from studies investigating the association between locus of control and underachievement (Kanoy 1980; Davis and Connell 1985; McClelland et al. 1991). Two of these studies found intergroup differences but in different directions, and the third study showed no differences between the groups. However, Bender (1987) reviewed studies of children with learning difficulties and concluded that the majority of the studies suggest a link between external locus of control and learning disability. Nunn and Parish (1992) have shown that pupils who are considered to be at risk of educational failure have developed more external views of themselves and are more anxious, have lower self-esteem and exhibit more symptoms of depression than more successful pupils, who in turn were more internal in their locus of control. Given the above evidence, it is clearly possible that if children believe that they are responsible for their learning and have some control over their success, they may also believe that it is worth trying harder to improve their performance.

Before going on to consider the role of the family in the development of locus of control, it is worth noting that Nunn (1988) found significant relationships between internal locus of control and perceptions of adjustment in family, school and peer relationships. Higher internality was associated with more positive relationships in all three contexts. Nunn hypothesises that since internal locus of control is positively related to achievement, behaviours which are consistent with internality lead to greater task persistence and achievement at school, which is associated with greater perceived adjustment.

Locus of control and the family

There is much evidence that children develop positive or negative self-esteem mainly according to what they learn about themselves from significant others (parents), so likewise it would seem reasonable to hypothesise that the antecedents of locus of control may also be found in the child–parent relationship. Thus, when addressing the internal attributions of self-esteem and locus of control, it is necessary, in a systemic framework, to consider these characteristics in the context of the wider systems of the child's world, specifically the family and the school.

The relationship between locus of control and family circumstances has been addressed by Rotter (1966), Epstein and Komorita (1971), Rollins and Thomas (1979) and Lau and Leung (1992). Most have explored children's current perceptions of family relationships, and some draw upon older populations' memories of childhood experiences and contexts. All of these studies have concluded that poor parent–child relations and inconsistent discipline are related to external locus of control. Lau and Leung studied the relationship between Chinese adolescents' self-concept, delinquency and relations with parents and school, and their perception of personal control from a multidimensional perspective. Results showed that external control was associated with low general academic and social self-concepts, high delinquency and poor relations with parents and school. Gender differences were found, with girls' sense of external control being more strongly associated with their poor relationships with parents and school, their appearance and friendships. Boys' sense of external control was more strongly associated with general behaviour and social acceptance.

Parenting influences on development of locus of control

In Crandall's (1973) longitudinal study of locus of control measures in young adulthood, results showed that mothers of 'internals' were more likely to have 'pushed their children towards independence, less often rewarded dependency, and displayed less intense involvement and contact with them'. She says it may be that warm, protective, supportive maternal behaviour is necessary for the assumption of personal responsibility during childhood, but that in the long run it may militate against internality at maturity. This rather smacks of the 'cruel to be kind' maxim, which, we suggest, can only result positively if seen in the context of Fromm's (1956) distinction between 'babying' and 'nurturing'. Fromm says that in motherly love the relationship between the two persons involved is one of inequality; the child is helpless and dependent on the mother. In order for it to grow, it must become more independent, until it does not need the mother any more.

This mother–child relationship is paradoxical, and requires the most intense love on the mother's part, and yet this love must help the child to grow away from the mother to become fully independent. Crandall explains that the 'push from the nest' is helpful for the development of an internal locus of control as its function is to put the child into a more active intercourse with its physical and social environment, so that there is more opportunity for it to observe the effect of its own behaviour, and the ensuing events, unmediated by maternal intervention.

Nowicki and Segal (1974) conducted a study with 112 high school students to ascertain perceived parental behaviour associated with locus of control orientation. Broadly, the results showed that perceived maternal nurturance was found to be associated with male internality, and all subjects perceived parents as having somewhat similar locus of control orientation to their own. Participants' expressed internality was associated with higher achievement for males, and with greater social involvement for females. Perceived parental internality was significantly associated with greater female achievement. Nowicki and Segal suggest from their results that locus of control may mean different things to males and females, and that internal females may obtain higher grades not because they learn more but because they are more aware than boys of the social behaviours which lead to higher grade points. In a later study Nowicki and Duke (1979) concluded that internality is related to particular paternal characteristics of understanding, tolerance, helping and contact seeking and to an open family climate.

Influences of family size and birth order

Parenting is not the only aspect of family circumstances that studies have investigated. Morin (1983) has reviewed studies of birth order and family size, noting that those which relate to locus of control have produced mixed results. Crandall *et al.* (1965) found first-born children to be more internal, while Eswara (1978) found first-borns to be more external. The most significant difference was between the first-born and middle-born children, and there was no significant difference between first- and last-born children. Eswara's work suggests that due to inexperience parents might act more inconsistently towards first-born children, which produces a greater dependency and subsequently a greater tendency to externality. Any significant difference between the first- and last-born depended upon the space between the last-born and the next child up in the family. Last-borns who were three or more years younger than the next child showed no difference from the first-borns. This may be explained by the possibility that the last-born receive a great deal of attention not just from parents but from older siblings. Through this additional attention the last-borns may become dependent on others and upon external forces.

Alder (1964) is mindful that it is not only birth order in the numerical sense but the psychological situation of the child in the family which may be influential. For example, being the first-born child to survive is different from being the first-born or the first conceived; the first-born boy may hold a different family position from the first-born child. As Elliott (1993) points out: 'Quantitative analysis of birth order positions may not prove sufficiently sensitive to differentiate between the differing experiences of family members.' He further points out that there is a strong correlation between family size and socio-economic deprivation, which may also confuse the findings.

Traumatic family experiences and locus of control

Several studies have considered the effects of traumatic family experiences upon the development of locus of control in children. Duke and Lancaster (1976) found that children raised in families where the father was absent tended to be more external than children raised in families where the father was present. Generally the literature supports the conclusion that children who have experienced traumatic family circumstances, such as divorce, serious illness or bereavement, tend to exhibit external locus of control. However, yet again, the literature and evidence is contradictory. Katler *et al.* (1984) found children who had experienced divorce had a greater degree of internality than children from families where there had been no divorce. Katler *et al.* offer a complicated explanation for this, saying that there is a tendency for children to assume blame and responsibility for the divorce, or alternatively children might experience a need to engage in highly organised mastery activities as a means of countering feelings of powerlessness in the face of divorce.

Davis and Connell (1985) conducted two exploratory studies involving children's reports of parental behaviour and parents' child rearing and internal–external control attitudes as antecedents of children's beliefs that the reinforcements they receive are a consequence of their own behaviour (internals). Internals were more likely than externals to report their parents as showing more positive involvement and consistent discipline, and less rejection, hostile control and withdrawal of relations. There were no direct relationships between children's internal–external beliefs and parents' child rearing and internal–external attitudes. However, parents whose children had an internal–external orientation similar to their own expressed less disciplinarian and more indulgent child-rearing attitudes than parents whose children had an internal–external belief unlike their own. Parent–child internal–external similarity may be mediated by nurturing accepting parental behaviour.

Locus of control and the school

As presented earlier in this chapter, Jersild (1952) emphasises the importance of school in the lives of children, describing it as second only to home in respect of its influence upon children's development. It is therefore reasonable to expect that what happens to children in school will influence where they locate locus of control – either towards internality or towards externality. However, there has been little investigation into the relationship between locus of control and school type. The Coleman Report (1966) is a composite of several surveys conducted by a large number of social scientists investigating the relationship of school achievement to a variety of factors, including personality measures of children. Among the many findings it was stated that a 'pupil attitudinal factor, which appears to have a stronger relationship to achievement than all the school factors together, is the extent to which an individual feels he has some control over his destiny' with teachers often referring to disruptive pupils as having 'an attitude problem' and 'being out of control'.

Locus of control and emotional and behavioural difficulties

Several studies (e.g. Coggins 1984; Nunn and Parish 1992) have demonstrated that children with emotional and/or behavioural difficulties (EBD) score significantly more externally than a population of non-EBD children. A number of other studies have attempted to compare children's locus of control scores with problems of behaviour and adjustment as reported by the children themselves.

There are also studies that have found no association between externality and adjustment difficulties with EBD and non-EBD populations. Kendall *et al.* (1976) found no significant difference in externality between groups of emotionally disturbed and normally developing boys. Of relevance when attempting to make sense of the difference in outcome of these studies is a consensus of definition of the term 'emotional and behaviourally disturbed'. Galloway and Goodwin (1987) argue that labels such as disturbed, disruptive, maladjusted, which are often used to describe pupils, bear little relationship to specific behaviours. Such labels suggest within-child explanations for certain unacceptable behaviours. In this study we do not use such labels, nor do we assume that all pupils who have been permanently excluded from school would appropriately be described as emotionally and/or behaviourally disturbed. This is contrary to Sanders (1990) who chose formal exclusion from school as an administrative criterion for selecting a population of disruptive pupils. The discrete population for the present study is determined by fact (i.e. the fact that they have been permanently excluded from school). The subjectivity lies in who or what determined the criteria for these exclusions.

Locus of control and self-esteem

Epstein and Komorita (1971) evaluated personality and situational parameters relating to internal–external control by investigating self-esteem and success–failure variables with 20 subjects. The results confirmed that experiences of failure rather than of success were attributed to external causes, and high self-esteem subjects were more internal than low self-esteem or moderate self-esteem subjects. These results suggest that it may be possible to cushion the belief in one's powerlessness by the development of a positive self-concept and self-esteem.

Results of our assessment of locus of control

We used the Nowicki-Strickland Locus of Control Scale for Children (CNSIE) as our measure of locus of control. Based on Rotter's adult scales, it is designed for use by boys and girls between the ages of 8 and 18 years and is the most widely employed generalised locus of control scale for children, used now in over one thousand studies in a dozen different language communities. Given the literature review presented, we predicted that the excluded group would show more external locus of control than the comparison group. Results were analysed using Mann-Whitney tests, which showed the excluded group to be significantly more external than the comparison group ($z = -3.5$, $p < .001$) and the comparison group to be significantly more internal than the excluded ($z = -3.0$, $p < .002$), in line with our prediction.

This result is of major significance to how parents and education-alists understand pupils' motivation for their challenging and undesirable behaviour. External locus of control may provide a modus operandi for such pupils, whereby they do not feel that they are either responsible for their actions or for events which happen to them. They are likely to hold the view that something or someone else is responsible for their responses to a situation, which led to them getting into trouble. This leads to two possible outcomes: first, that these pupils react instinctively, without considering their part in the cause and effect of behaviours; or second, that these pupils easily and readily 'blame' others, not maliciously but because they genuinely believe that they themselves cannot be responsible. This will be further illustrated in consideration of data from the interviews with the children from the excluded group. The excluded pupils, in their reports of the incidents which led to their final exclusion from school, talked in terms of responding and reacting to other people rather than being proactive in an incident. Teachers and parents often reported the same incident in a different way, believing that the pupil was not merely reacting, but had in most cases 'caused' and initiated the event.

Those pupils in the excluded group who had taken part in social skills programmes (in three cases, whilst at the pupil referral unit, post-exclusion), and who all show high scores for external locus of control were reported by their teachers as being 'very good' in the role-play activities, where they acted out appropriate responses to incidents which they had encountered and found difficult in the school context. However, when these pupils encountered similar incidents in the PRU but outside the role-play exercise, they returned to their earlier inappropriate responses. This returns us to Phares's example of Karl S, whose inability to profit from didactic intervention led to the development of locus of control theory. It would seem that, like Karl S, our excluded pupils had not been able to alter their 'real' behaviour, perhaps because they remained unable to acknowledge their own influence upon events.

Case study examples of external and internal locus of control

It was evident in our interviews with the excluded pupils that, to some extent, they were able to identify in themselves feelings of loss of control and power, and an inability to effect changes in their situation. Where they had encountered events such as divorce, serious illness, separation, and of course school exclusion, they felt that they had been given no choice and had no power to effect change and/or alter the outcome of events which directly affected them. The following extract is taken from our interview with 15-year-old David, whose mother and stepfather had divorced when he was 13.

David   *[excluded pupil, high external, low internal locus of control scores]*: I didn't want my Mum and Pete to split up but I couldn't do anything about it could I? I liked Pete and he said we'd still see each other so I wasn't too worried and thought it would be OK. But my Mum didn't want me to see him so now I don't know where he is. I suppose I don't really feel that I have any choice really . . . and I knew that when I went to that meeting you know at school with those people they'd made up their minds and it didn't matter what I said . . . they were going to kick me out no matter what my Mum and me said . . . it was a waste of time going.

In this extract David is talking about his feelings of lack of control when describing both a domestic (family) event and a school (exclusion meeting with the school governors) event. Children do not exhibit external locus of control in some contexts and not in others. David acknowledges that in the matter of his continuing to see his stepfather it was his mother who made the decision, yet in the matter of the school exclusion he reports that it did not matter what his mother said as 'they'd made up their minds'. This suggests that, in the hierarchy of influence, David saw himself as being the least able to influence the outcome of events. In the home his mother wielded the greatest influence, and at school it was the school governors. Where school matters were concerned, David presents a belief that all power lies within the school and that neither he nor even his mother can affect the outcome of events or decisions.

This theme is repeated throughout the interviews with the excluded pupils. The following extracts are from interviews with an excluded pupil, Jade, and a comparison pupil, Jane. They were both asked to describe an event they could remember happening in the family which had been upsetting or worrying.

Jade *[excluded pupil, high external, low internal locus of control scores]*: Well right I was living with my Dad then he got a new girlfriend who didn't want me to live there so my Dad said that I had to live with my Mum but she said that my Step-Dad couldn't afford for me to live there so I went to a children's home (. . .) which was OK but then my social worker said that I had to come here to my Mum. Then Mum said that I could choose what school to go to but the Town Hall said that I had to go to (X) school but I didn't want to 'cause I heard it was rubbish but I had to go anyway and they didn't want me and I didn't want them and then they kicked me out anyway . . .

Jane *[comparison pupil, low external, high internal locus of control scores]*: I had wanted to go to (Y) school and we were told that it was full. Anyway I was really upset coz all my friends were going there so my Mum and Dad rang the Headmaster Mr (A) and he said that we could go for an interview. So we all went and he said that I could have the next place. If we hadn't gone to meet him I don't think I would have got in. My Mum and Dad helped a lot but Mr (A) said that I had shown him how badly I wanted to go to this school.

The differences in these two descriptions demonstrate differences between internal and external locus of control. In the first extract Jade describes her father's girlfriend as initiating her removal from home. She then describes her mother's husband (her stepfather) deciding that he could not afford for Jade to live with him and her mother. Jade continues by describing her social worker as deciding that she should, after all, live with her mother and stepfather. When it came to a choice of school, for the first time in this extract Jade describes being given a choice by her mother, but then reports that this choice was withdrawn by the LEA who decided which school she would attend. At no time in this extract does Jade refer to being in a position to influence either where or with whom she lives, or where she is able to go to school.

In the second extract Jane describes that she was not initially able to attend the school of her choice at secondary transfer. She describes her parents responding to the fact that she was upset by this and that they took a proactive role in telephoning and then meeting the head teacher of the school. Jane also describes how she was able to let the head teacher know how much she wanted to attend his school and how they were able to secure a place. Jane's account demonstrates her acknowledgement that she can influence and affect her parents' behaviour to 'fight' for her and support her as well as her being able to influence the head teacher.

Sadly, in our study we did not attempt to assess the locus of control of the parents or teachers. This would have been relevant and of interest, since, just as the excluded group overwhelmingly felt that external events and forces prevented them from influencing events in their lives, so it is probable that the adults working with these pupils will have similar feelings. Indeed there are clues to this from the interviews with head teachers and from the school ethos questionnaires completed by teachers and parents, which we report in the chapter on school factors.

Summary

The data presented in this section support the view that the excluded pupils in this study experience significantly more difficulties in their cognitive ability and reading and spelling ability than the matched comparison pupils. Yet only one pupil in the study (an excluded pupil) had a Statement of Special Educational Needs and he was of well above average cognitive and literacy ability and had a statement identifying EBD. The two pupils in the comparison group who were identified in the study as experiencing learning difficulties had both been referred to the educational psychologist by the school (100 per cent), whereas six of the excluded group identified in the study as experiencing similar levels of difficulty had been referred prior to their exclusion from school (30 per cent) but only two of these had been referred by the school (10 per cent). This is interesting as it implies that schools are of the view that behaviour *causes* learning problems, that is, they make a causal attribution and so do not refer pupils whose learning problems they feel they understand the reasons for.

The excluded group did not differ from the comparison group in athletic, romantic, physical appearance, job or social acceptance self-esteem scores on the Harter scales. There were significant differences between the groups for behaviour, scholastic, close friendship and global self-esteem with the excluded pupils showing lower scores in these domains than the comparison pupils. It is important to note the strong relationship which scholastic, behaviour and job self-esteem have to the school and academic context. With respect to support from parents and teachers, the excluded group felt significantly less supported than the comparison pupils. The excluded pupils demonstrated a significant difference from the comparison group in respect of locus of control, with the excluded group being highly external.

Relationships between attainment, self-esteem and locus of control

The results of the present study relating to the within-child variables of cognitive ability, self-esteem and locus of control, and the inter-relationship between these three subsystems demonstrate that the excluded pupils were significantly less able in their cognitive ability than the comparison pupils, especially in their verbal skills. Children who are less able and demonstrate poorer achievement than other pupils are less likely to feel in control of the outcomes of events relating to ability, and are likely to develop an external locus of control. The self-esteem data of the present study supports the inter-relationship of the three subsystems in that the excluded group showed significantly lower self-esteem for behaviour, scholastic and global self-esteem, relating directly, one can assume, to school achievement. Therefore in systemic terms a circular causality can be identified (Figure 3.1).

In 14 cases parents of the excluded pupils reported no behaviour difficulties with their child at home. Outside the school context, where academic ability can take a lower priority than in the school context, where achievement in areas of practical rather than verbal skills, and youth culture activities such as dancing, rollerblading, graffiti drawing, and knowledge of popular music are valued, self-esteem was

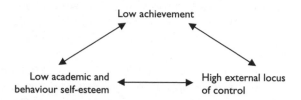

Figure 3.1 Relationships between three variables

shown to be no different for the excluded and comparison pupils. This supports the work of Coopersmith (1967) who recognised that high self-esteem can be the result of performing well in specific areas other than those relating to school achievement. Those studies which report low self-esteem in excluded pupils are accurate to a point but do not give the whole picture and, unlike our own study, do not have the benefit of comparison with a matched group of non-excluded pupils. Coopersmith also proposed:

> Children with high self-esteem are likely to be considerable sources of travail and disturbance to their parents, teachers and other persons in authority . . . persons whose behaviour may be viewed by those in authority as disruptive . . . are generally more capable of protecting their interests and opinions than are persons who take a less favourable view of themselves.
>
> Coopersmith (1967: 321)

This somewhat counterintuitive proposal is interesting in the light of our results, with excluded pupils showing preservation of high self-esteem in certain areas of the self. It is possible that the very fact that children have some positive self-esteem (not necessarily in the areas of behaviour or academic self-esteem) may provide them with a greater confidence to protect their own interests and opinions in the face of authority figures. In other words, a positive self-esteem may be a prerequisite for assertiveness and 'sticking up for oneself'. What is clear in the present study is that the low self-esteem of the excluded pupils is likely to have some connection with negative influences of school systems upon within-child systems. It is also interesting that disruptive behaviour in school was not necessarily associated with disruptive behaviour at home. This tempts us to speculate that the excluded pupils' low self-esteem in key areas of the self which are most highly valued by the school system led to them feeling angry, upset and frustrated for much of the time in school. Their positive self-esteem in other areas of the self served to motivate them to protect themselves against these feelings by becoming disruptive and refusing to accept the school's values. As the excluded pupils were valued more holistically by their families, the same negative feelings were less likely to be engendered in the home situation. This relates to the ecosystem work of Cooper and Upton (1991) where behaviour is described as the product of ongoing interactions between influences in the social (school) environment and the internal motivations which derive from prior experience.

Parents often described their children as being different at home from how they were described by the school, which suggests that pupils place a boundary between home life (the family system) and school life (the school system). None of the parents of the excluded pupils reported that school had sought their advice about how to manage their children's behaviour. The parents felt that when they reported that their children were well behaved at home they were not believed by schools. Teachers often reacted with surprise when pupils who were generally disruptive in school behaved with maturity and responsibility on school trips, away from the school setting. The boundary between the family systems and the school systems was strongly drawn and completely impermeable.

In the following chapter, we turn to a consideration of the family system. We shall return to the child system in Chapter 7, where we try to illuminate the connections between the three systems of child, family and school.

Chapter 4

Understanding the families

Risk and resilience

> Children are invariably born into a social network, typically a family. The family, too, is embedded in a social system. The family, the primary institution responsible for transforming societal maintenance and perception goals into directions for the new individuals, is thus at the core of socialisation. Hence the family is society's adaptional unit.
>
> (Lerner and Spanier 1978: 214)

In our study we compared within-family variables of the excluded and comparison groups of children. As we will show in discussing relevant literature, there is evidence that children from 'high-risk' families are the most vulnerable to school exclusion. However, not all children from high-risk families have adverse outcomes in terms either of their school careers or their subsequent lives. We therefore investigated not only risk factors, but also protective factors that help make children resilient to risk. In this chapter, we discuss the role of the family in preparing children for the inevitable ups and downs of life, with particular reference to the family's role in fostering children's ability to adapt to school life. We also discuss several recognised sources of family stress that can lead to children being at risk of adverse outcomes. We then discuss the concept of resilience, and the factors that foster resilience in children. This is followed by a description of the data we obtained from interviews with parents of excluded and comparison children, and the ways in which the information from these interviews was organised into various themes. Finally, we suggest that families of the excluded children differed systematically from those of the comparison children, and illustrate these suggestions with material from the interviews.

The family as preparation for life

Children grow up in families embedded in networks of social relationships and much of what they learn is about their social world. They learn about people and how to anticipate their behaviour, and about how people's behaviours vary according to their needs and circumstances. They also learn about themselves, what kind of people they are, how others respond to them, what it means to be a boy or a girl, a member of a minority or a majority ethnic group, to be able bodied or disabled, sick or healthy. Children's families and social networks serve as both the world that they inhabit and as the world about which they are constantly learning.

Family relationships are intrinsically charged with emotion – for example, love and affection, anger, envy, sadness, despair, aggression, rivalry all find expression to a greater or lesser degree within the context of 'the family'. While children love their parents, they can also feel anger towards them, and struggle hard to resist parental control. While parents love their children, they can also feel frustration, anger and despair as they watch their children acquire habits of which they disapprove, and develop ways and behaviours that they dislike. These of course can be behaviours that parents uncomfortably recognise as their own.

The familiar and emotional exchanges between family members (parents, children, siblings, grandparents) provide a forum for children to gain a practical grasp of some of the causes of distress, anger, happiness, etc. in other family members, and of the demands and rules that operate in their families, which may or may not be mirrored in the wider world.

Families vary considerably, for example, whether there are one or both parents still living, one or two parents living together with their children, whether the adults have paid employment, adequate accommodation. The experiences of parents and children and how they feel about themselves and each other are influenced by the kinds of family in which they live.

The family and adaptation to school

When children start school they begin to live in separate but inter-related worlds, with the family continuing to provide a central context for development. For many children, contact with the outside world starts early with child-care arrangements (with professional carers or grandparents) and attendance at playschools or nursery classes. Going to school allows children to become more independent, although parents continue to control the major aspects of their children's lives. Parents are expected to prepare their children for the wider world. This includes how to behave appropriately in certain circumstances. Schools expect that children will have learned from their families how to obey rules, and how to modify their behaviour to suit a variety of situations, many of them unfamiliar to the young child. Children who behave 'badly' within the confines of their own family may be forgiven, and will continue to be loved and will know this. This may not be the case if the unacceptable behaviour takes place outside the family, where such behaviour may lead to the child being publicly reprimanded or even rejected. Unacceptable behaviour in a school setting can be used as an example for other children, thus amplifying the publicity for the child.

As children become more used to school they move between one world (the family) and the other (school), usually but not always keeping each world in touch with the other. Some parents strive to know more about their child's other world by involving themselves in activities such as playing an active part in the parent–teacher association, becoming a parent governor, befriending teachers. Other parents actively avoid such engagement, preferring to keep their distance. This preference for distance can be misunderstood by professionals who sometimes misinterpret it as parents showing a lack of interest in their children's education.

The time when young children first start school and leave their families for a large part of the day can be a testing time not only for the children but also for their families (especially mothers). Some mothers miss the companionship of their children, and the day-to-day routine and structure which having a child at home can impose. Teachers begin to take the place of parents during the school day, in terms of taking control of the child's safety, comforts and education, and taking over the authority role. Children begin to realise that adults outside their family sometimes have different values and expectations from those with which they have been brought up. This can provide a source of conflict and confusion for the child. The ways in which parents prepare their children for school, their own values and attitudes towards education, and their expectations of and support for their children's developing competence and educational achievement, all influence children's performance at school, particularly as measured by vocabulary, cognitive ability, reading ability, problem solving, exploratory behaviour and social competence (Weiner *et al.* 1992).

Sources of stress in families

Given that we all experience unfortunate and undesirable events in our lives at one time or another, it is important to have a sense of which stressful events are considered to put us particularly at risk. Risk factors can be described as being situations that increase the likelihood of people developing emotional and/or behavioural problems at some point in their lives. Broad categories of risk factors identified in previous research include early separation from mother (main carer), the bereavement of a close relative, divorce and family conflict, the serious illness of a family member, the absence of father. We discuss the first three of these in more detail below.

Early separation from mother (main carer)

Bowlby (1949) contended that early and prolonged separation of young children from their mothers was a prime cause of what he described as a delinquent character development and persistent misbehaviour. This is supported by the work of Beres and Obers (1950), who identified links between psychological problems in adolescents and their experiences of early maternal deprivation. Further support is found in work by Robertson and Robertson (1953) who concluded, from their seminal work with young children admitted as inpatients to hospital and separated from their mothers, that the signs of emotional loss and trauma the children showed resulted from the maternal separation rather than from the effects of their medical condition or treatment. As a result of these findings, additional visiting rights for parents of young children and, later, arrangements and facilities for parents to stay with their young children during hospitalisation were introduced.

However, the putative ill effects of early maternal separation are not universally accepted. For example, Rutter (1981) argues forcefully that separation from natural parents need not negate child–adult bonding. Upton (1981) concluded that neither separation per se, nor separation from a biological parent or permanent parent substitute, were key determinants of children's development of misbehaviour; of more importance is the quality of the substitute care. In terms of temporary separation, such as hospitalisation, Rutter argues that while temporary emotional distress may arise from such experiences, they are unlikely to have a lasting impact upon the child. However, it seems reasonable to assume that the more distressing the original cause that produced the situation of being separated, the more likely that the emotional distress arising from separation will have a lasting impact.

Stacey et al. (1970) found that any impact which hospitalisation had upon children depended upon their age at the time of the admission, length and frequency of the stay, temperamental characteristics of the children and their relationship with their mothers. They suggested that children experienced the greatest impact if the separation took place between six months and four years of age. They also found that repeated admission to hospital and longer stays were associated with increased risks of behaviour problems later in life. The most vulnerable children were those who experienced stress in the home prior to being admitted to hospital, or who already experienced feelings of insecurity upon admission to hospital.

This is supported by a study by Weiner et al. (1992), who identified differences among children admitted to hospital for an extended period of time, when their mothers were unable to stay with them. These differences depended upon the children's previous experiences of occasional routine separations from their mothers. Children without these experiences showed a greater degree of uncertainty, and were less able to understand what had happened to them than children who had been occasionally cared for by babysitters or child minders, in situations where they understood and knew the routines and were able to benefit from, rather than be traumatised by, the experience of separation.

Close family bereavement

Rutter (1981) found that bereaved children tended to manifest heightened shyness, timidity and withdrawal, as compared with children of divorced or separated parents, who tended to show aggressive and antisocial behaviour. Bowlby (1970) and Rotter (1966) suggest that immediate grief reactions are milder and shorter in duration in young children compared with those for adolescents. Differences in age are likely to be explained by differences in children's cognitive understanding. However, Rutter suggests that the apparent short-lived grief reactions of the younger age group often result in delayed consequences, sometimes in the form of psychiatric disorders later in life. He also acknowledges that these long-term effects are probably a result of the consequences which follow a bereavement (especially following the death of a parent) such as change of home, change of school, change of caregiver and the possible introduction of another family member such as a stepparent and step-siblings.

Divorce and family conflict

Inevitably divorce involves the disorganising and reorganising of families. Throughout the time of divorce, which can start many years before the actual physical separation of the parents, and can often be followed by many years of arguing and stress, children are likely to feel more vulnerable to other stresses which at a different time they may cope with easily. They may also feel less supported by their parents, who themselves may be concerned with their own emotional suffering. During this time children may need special help from their parents, at a time when their parents are least able to provide it.

There is a degree of confusion in the research literature, with different studies presenting different conclusions as to the nature of the impact of divorce on children. Children are most seriously affected if parental divorce occurs during a child's early years. Rutter (1971) found that children aged between two and three years were particularly vulnerable to the separation of their parents, especially when the leaving parent was of the same sex. However, Wallersten and Kelly (1980), whilst reporting that children's responses to parental divorce are modified by their age and level of development, with different patterns of coping emerging at different ages and levels, suggest that vulnerability does not seem to be markedly increased or decreased at any particular age.

Rutter (1971) reports that much of the stress experienced by children at the time of divorce is more the consequence of prior parental discord than of the parental separation itself. Jobling (1976) agrees that behaviour problems are not generated by the divorce itself but by the turbulent relationship between parents that led up to the separation and later divorce. This view might lead to the assumption that there can be positive outcomes of divorce, if this serves to resolve parental conflict, and, in cases like this, both children and parents have been known to acknowledge that the divorce has been a positive thing. However, research by Hetherington (1991) and Wallersten and Kelly (1980) shows that children do not report that their parents' divorce has served to resolve conflict with both parents tending to be inconsistent, less affectionate and lacking in control over their children in the immediate aftermath of divorce. During the first year after divorce, mothers often became depressed, self-involved, erratic, less supportive and ineffectually authoritarian with their children. Fathers tended to begin by being indulgent and permissive, but then increased restrictions and more often used negative sanctions when their children misbehaved.

Coleman *et al.* (1966) refers to children's behaviour problems as being consequent upon adverse conditions arising from relationships among other family members, as well as their relationships with either or both parents. In the case of divorce, children often feel that they need to show loyalty to one parent rather than the other, and siblings may hold conflicting views in terms of 'taking sides', thus creating conflict among other family members. This conflict is likely to permeate outside the immediate family and involve grandparents, aunts and uncles.

In their extensive work with children and parents who have experienced separation and divorce, Dowling and Gorell Barnes (2000) identified five aspects of divorce and separation that impact upon children's development and coping strategies. In their view, although divorce is an important risk factor for children's adjustment problems, there is much that parents can do to mitigate the negative consequences. It is important that children should have continuing secure relationships with parents or other caregivers to allow continued development of healthy emotional and social relationships. In these difficult stressful times, it is perhaps natural to feel unable to respond fully to children's demands. This may be easier for parents who understand that children's wish for proximity, attention and responsiveness is a developmental expression of their needs. As far as possible, parents need to be able to reassure children that they will be able to continue relationships with both parents, and to accept that their children's anger also stems from frustration of their wish for love and care.

As in the case of the death of a parent, Rutter acknowledges that long-term effects of divorce are probably a result of the consequences which follow, such as the possible introduction of another family member such as a step-parent and step-siblings. It is interesting to note here that step-families were significantly over-represented amongst the excluded pupils in Hayden's (1997) study of excluded pupils.

Impact of risk factors on children

Longitudinal studies (e.g. Cowen and Work 1988; Werner 1989) highlight the impact upon children of adverse family events such as family discord, separation and divorce, abuse and serious illness, with data collected from large numbers of individuals over a number of years. In Werner's study nearly 700 children were studied over a period of 40 years on the island of Kauai. These children were mostly from poor Japanese, Filipino, Hawaiian and mixed race families, with parents who were unskilled plantation workers. A third of the children were classified as 'at risk', the criterion for which was exposure to at least four risk factors (e.g. serious health problems, family violence, divorce and mental illness) before the age of two years. By the age of 18 years two-thirds of the 'at risk' group had, as predicted, done poorly. The behaviours exhibited by this group included being in trouble at school, in trouble with the law, in need of mental health services, early pregnancy. However, the remaining one-third of the 'at risk' group developed into 'competent, caring and confident young adults' (Werner 1989: 9). The cultural and ethnic differences between these children and the excluded and control pupils we worked with are considerable, but Werner's study is relevant to ours in that many of the risk factors experienced by the children of the Kauai study are similar to those experienced by some of the excluded and comparison pupils with whom we worked.

Rutter's (1976) study of 10 and 11 year olds on the Isle of Wight identified a small group of children who were described as being psychiatrically disturbed. These children were found to have poor concentration, were unpopular with other children and with adults, were restless and fidgety, aggressive, irritable, fearful and dishonest. They were more likely to be living in materially poor homes and overcrowded conditions than their peers, to have a mother with a history of psychiatric illness, a father with a criminal record, to have spent time in the care of the local authority, and to come from a discordant home. The children did not necessarily experience all of these events, but would have experienced at least two of them. Rutter concluded that each of these events carried equal weight, resulting in similar impact upon the child, and that it is the combination of events that leads to risk. He suggests that most children are able to cope effectively with at least two risk factors simultaneously, but that the presence of three or more risk factors almost always results in emotional and/or behavioural difficulties.

Relation between risk factors and school exclusion

Hayden (1997: 10) describes the 'wide range of debates and traditions upon which to draw when focusing upon family-based explanations of children's behaviour and ultimately their exclusion from school'. Her purpose in exploring some of these debates and traditions is to attempt to understand more fully how different family cultures might advantage or disadvantage children's capacity to cope with life's uncertainties, and to fulfil their potential as future adults and parents. Hayden's study of excluded primary school children reported that family tensions and difficulties were present in almost all of the cases studied. Her work provided strong evidence that a majority of pupils excluded from school were living in families about whom support services had major concerns, with 76 per cent of these families identified as having social services, child guidance or psychiatric service involvement. This level of involvement from support services is not replicated in our own study, although we do have evidence of a significant difference in the overall presence of stresses in the families of the excluded pupils compared with the families of comparison pupils. Hayden focused upon 11 of 37 life events using Chandler's (1981) Sources of Stress Inventory to identify risk factors in the families of excluded primary school children. The results showed that family breakdown was the most common stress factor present in this group of excluded pupils, with only 11 per cent of the children living at home with both natural parents. Nearly 61 per cent of the families had no form of paid employment, and 44 per cent of the children had spent some time in the care of the local authority during the school year in which they were excluded from school. This is a highly significant finding, but again not replicated in our study. We will discuss possible reasons for this later.

Galloway et al. (1982) also noted that the family circumstances of pupils excluded from school were frequently stressful, and that the incidence of serious illness and accident in the family were higher for these pupils than for pupils who had not been excluded from school.

The concept of resilience

Most children are likely to experience many potentially stressful life events as they grow up, and the majority of children who experience divorce, bereavement, serious and chronic family illness or personal illness, or special educational needs do not develop challenging or antisocial and unacceptable behaviours which result in school exclusion. In our study, when we compared the presence of risk factors between the excluded and comparison groups we found only two individual risk factors that were significantly more likely to be present in the families of the excluded pupils. There was thus reason to believe that the comparison children, and their families, were perhaps more resilient and better able to cope with the challenges life inevitably poses. We now discuss the concept of resilience, and factors that influence its development. The notion of 'family resilience' is relatively new, and can be defined as follows:

> Family resilience describes the path a family follows as it adapts and prospers in the face of stress, both in the present and over time. Resilient families respond positively to these conditions in unique ways, depending upon the context, developmental level, the interactive combination of risk and protective factors, and the family's shared outlook.
>
> (Hawley and DeHann 1996: 293)

This definition suggests that resilient families adapt to stressful events and circumstances, and may even feel stronger as a result. Resilient family members will report being closer as a result of a traumatic event. Rutter (1985) says that the quality of resilience resides in how people deal with life changes and what they do about their situations. It is therefore likely that the long-term effects of stressful life events will depend upon how they are dealt with at the time and over time. In this context, Antonovsky (1987) developed the concept of 'coherence', which McCubbin et al. (1980) defined as being a shared world view expressing the family's feelings of confidence towards the future. Antonovsky also emphasised the importance of what he termed 'comprehensibility': that is, the degree to which individuals have a cognitive understanding of events. These concepts of coherence and comprehensibility turned out to be very important markers of resilience in the families in our study. As we show later, in presenting data from family interviews, the ways in which families recounted and made sense of stressful events differed among families of excluded and comparison children. We therefore agree with Rutter (1988), who argues that both risk and protective factors are largely inert on their own, but often serve as catalysts and buffers for stressful events. It is impossible to make assumptions or predictions based solely upon knowledge of certain events, which may be considered to be risk events, without understanding how these events interact with other life circumstances. Once again, it is the interrelations between systems and subsystems that matter. Risk and protective factors need to be examined in the contexts within which they exist, rather than assumptions made that any particular event or characteristic will inevitably put someone at risk or serve to protect them.

Factors that foster resilience in children

Rutter and Giller (1983) led the way in attempting to delineate the factors that promote the development of resilience in children. Several subsequent studies have examined this, usually by implementing longitudinal studies that follow up children identified as at high risk of adverse outcomes on the basis of the kinds of risk factors discussed earlier. Children who have positive outcomes despite the early presence of risk factors are deemed to be resilient. From these studies, resilient children are said to exhibit a sense of warmth, to be able to think through situations and act reflectively rather than impulsively, to have a feeling of control over their responses to life (which links clearly to our own findings of the importance of locus of control), to have mothers with positive experiences of their own schooling, and to have caring adults in their lives with whom they identify and who act as good role models (Henley 1993). These findings are echoed in a longitudinal study by Werner and Smith (1982), in which a third of children identified as being at high risk demonstrated no serious difficulties in later life. Three broad factors were identified as offering the greatest protection against subsequent serious psychiatric and/or social difficulties: qualities within the child (such as positive personality dispositions), a supportive family environment, and access to social support agencies. Similar findings were made by Kolvin et al. (1988), who showed that boys brought up in disadvantaged conditions and initially considered to be at risk of developing problems in later life, in fact did not develop the predicted difficulties. Kolvin et al. suggest that close parental care and positive social experiences during the first five years of life, good adult supervision from 5 to 10 years of age, and good cognitive development and progress at school between the ages of 10 and 15 years had provided protection.

Jenkins and Smith (1990) in their work with children living in disharmonious homes identified similar protective factors: good parent–child relationships (particularly between mother and child); good relationships with other family members, including siblings and grandparents; school competence; within-child factors such as an easy temperament and good cognitive ability; a close relationship with an adult outside the family; good quality relationships with other children; and the presence of a 'best friend'. Hawley and De Haan (1996) suggest that families in which there is what they describe as a 'good fit' between parents and child (again emphasising the mother–child relationship), which maintain family rituals and routines and exhibit proactive confrontation of problems, in which there has been minimal conflict in the home during infancy and an absence of divorce during adolescence, best promote qualities of resilience in children.

Schools can also foster resilience. As long ago as 1945, Wills suggested that pupils who carry burdens of past troubles often find difficulty communicating feelings of regret in a way that is easily recognised or socially appropriate. Caspari (1976) says that teachers' knowledge of adverse and stressful family circumstances will increase their understanding of the child's behaviour and will influence their reactions towards the child. Knowledge and understanding of sources of stress can also help to prevent the unintentional reproduction of the domestic traumas in the school setting. Hanko (1994) has described how trauma such as rejection and abandonment can so easily be unintentionally evoked in the school context. Bastide (1972) notes that if children's behaviour is to be changed, it is necessary to avoid reproducing or re-enacting the domestic stresses and attitudes that may have contributed to their present difficulties. Bastide suggests that teachers' understanding of these children needs to be strong enough to withstand whatever havoc the pupil can create. It is interesting to consider these suggestions in the light of our discussion of school ethos in Chapter 5. We might be tempted to speculate that incorporative schools, those in Parson's (1999) terms which adopt a more social democratic humanist approach to the functions of education and have a more holistic view of their role as educators, should offer an environment that is more able to facilitate the development of resilience. As we will see, in our study the schools with this kind of broad approach tended to resist excluding pupils, excluded fewer pupils for shorter time periods, and tended to see the decision to exclude as a failure on the part of the school.

It is interesting that all the studies cited above have identified protective factors that cross boundaries between the linked systems of within-child, within-family and within-institution factors, and thus emphasise the explanatory importance of adopting a systemic approach. This is particularly evident in the emphasis found in the writings of those concerned with the role of the school in promoting resilience, where knowledge and understanding of family factors is seen as essential: the boundary between home and school needs to be permeable for this knowledge and consequent understanding to develop.

Assessment of family risk factors in the study

These data were obtained from sections of the semi-structured interviews we carried out with parents of children in the excluded and comparison groups. We shall first describe the conditions under which the interviews were conducted and the data analysed and interpreted, before going on to present the results. The purpose of the study was first discussed with the parents and we assured them of confidentiality. Permission was sought and obtained in each case to taperecord the interviews. All names have been changed in the rich description of data that we present later.

Parents of excluded children were told the interview would be in four parts. First there was an opportunity to tell the story of the exclusion – parents' recollections of what happened, what kind of support they received and from where that support came, their hopes and expectations for what will happen to their child now. They were then asked about the developmental, medical and educational history of their child, followed by a social and medical history of the family, including the family structure, and information of any other family members who may have been excluded from school. Finally the parents were asked about their own memories of school. The interviews with the parents of children in the comparison group were identical except that they obviously did not include questions relating to the child's exclusion from school.

All parents, whether or not they were living at home with their child, were invited to participate in the semi-structured interviews. Where there were two parents or a parent and a step-parent living at home, both were invited to be interviewed. Mothers/stepmothers and fathers/stepfathers were interviewed together, but not in the presence of the pupil. Ideally we would have preferred to have been alone with the parents. However, due to difficult and cramped accommodation

in some of the homes this was not always possible, and some interviews took place in the presence of other family members, including
crying babies, barking dogs, and in one case a family friend. In every
case we were able to request that the television was switched off
during the interview. Where others were present during the interview,
they were asked not to contribute to the interview or to answer the
questions asked. We were often left with the feeling that listening to
the parents' responses to our questions was the first time that other
family members had heard details of the exclusion, the family
history and the parents' own memories and experiences of school.

We would have liked to match the socio-economic status of the
parents across the two groups. This proved not to be possible for
two reasons. First, information about socio-economic status of the
parents of the excluded group was obtained only during the semi-
structured interviews, and it was not possible accurately to establish
the socio-economic status of parents in advance of meeting with
them, as the schools did not keep such information. The second
reason is connected to the difficulties we experienced in securing a
comparison group of children matched for what we considered to be
the most important variables of age, gender, ethnicity and school:
requiring socio-economic status match of parents would have made
this even more difficult. However, this is clearly an important variable, as we were interested in testing out a general assumption that
excluded pupils are more likely to come from homes in the lower
socio-economic groups.

Socio-economic status of both groups of parents was determined
using the Registrar General's 'social class based on occupation', and
appeared similar across the two groups. Of the excluded group, two
parents were in managerial occupations, five in skilled occupations,
three in semi-skilled occupations and ten were either unskilled or
unemployed. Of the comparison group, two were in managerial
occupations, nine in skilled occupations, three in semi-skilled
occupations and six were either unskilled or unemployed.

Family structures differed in some respects across the two groups.
In both groups most (excluded, 19) or all (comparison, 20) pupils
lived with their natural mothers, with one excluded pupil living with
her stepmother. However, comparison children were more likely than
excluded children to live with their natural father (5 excluded children compared with 13 comparison children). Conversely, excluded
children were more likely than comparison children to live with a
stepfather (seven excluded children compared with two comparison

children). Among the excluded group, eight mothers and one father described themselves as single parents; no parents of comparison children described themselves in this way. Fathers of excluded children were much less likely to be present at interview than fathers of comparison children.

Although it might appear that accurate information (regarding with whom the pupils lived) should be available from the school, in 12 cases of the excluded pupils, and 5 cases of the comparison pupils, the school did not have accurate information. Family circumstances seemed to change sometimes suddenly, and parents and pupils do not always inform the school of such changes.

To make sense of the information provided in the interviews, two experienced educational psychologists from neighbouring education authorities listened to tapes of each interview. They were asked to identify the presence or absence of evidence of eight risk factors (divorce, early maternal separation, family conflict, serious illness of child, serious illness of close relative, death of close relative, absence of father in early childhood, serious illness of parent) in the material of each interview. We describe in detail the coding methods used to assess family resilience later in this chapter.

Given the high rate of family risk factors found in previous studies of exclusion, we expected the excluded group to show a high incidence of family risk factors. As previous studies have not included matched comparison groups, we were interested to see whether family risk factors were *more* prevalent in the families of excluded children than in families of comparison children, as this seems to be an underlying assumption of many previous studies.

Results of family risk assessment

Overall, the incidence of risk factors was greater in the families of excluded pupils than in the families of the comparison pupils, supporting the findings from previous studies (Table 4.1). However, although each single risk factor was consistently more likely to be present in families of children in the excluded group, these differences only reached statistical significance for two risk factors, early maternal separation, and serious illness of a parent. There was no significant difference between the groups in the cases of divorce, family conflict, serious illness of pupil or close relative other than a parent, death of a close relative and absence of father in early childhood. It is possible that with a larger sample significant differences might

Table 4.1 Number of children experiencing each risk factor, showing significant differences between groups

Risk factor	Excluded	Comparison	χ^2	p
Total	65	33		
Divorce	9	6	0.96	ns
Early maternal separation	10	3	5.6	<.02
Family conflict	10	6	1.7	ns
Serious illness of pupil	11	8	0.9	ns
Serious illness of close relative	5	2	1.5	ns
Death of close relative	4	2	0.8	ns
Absence of father in early childhood	10	6	1.7	ns
Serious illness of parent	6	0	7.1	<.01

have been apparent. However, our data does reflect the fact that many children now live in divorced, separated or reconstituted families, and the comparison group, not matched for family structure or constitution, represented similar profiles to the excluded group in this respect, with relatively high rates of divorce, family conflict, absence of father in early childhood, and serious illness of pupil.

However, pupils in the excluded group were likely to have experienced more risk factors than children in the comparison group. Two excluded pupils (Nicola and Terry) live in families where all eight of the identified risk factors are present. In one case (Kevin) six risk factors are present, Craig experienced five risk factors, Warren and Simon four, and Sarah and Matt experienced three each. For only one excluded pupil (Kharm) were no family risk factors identified. Two comparison pupils (Guy and Jamie) each experienced four risk factors, and Chris experienced three. No family risk factors were identified for three pupils in the comparison group.

The results for the excluded group would seem to support Rutter *et al.*'s (1979) conclusion that children are able to cope effectively with at least two risk factors but that the presence of three or more usually will result in emotional and/or behaviour difficulties. However, it seemed to us interesting that three of the comparison pupils had experienced three or more risk factors, and yet were reported as not having emotional or behaviour difficulties, and seven of the excluded group had experienced two or fewer risk factors, and yet had been excluded from school. We will consider later in this chapter the protective factors that might have led to some families and children being more resilient than others. Here, we shall turn to a rich presentation of the ways in which the two risk factors that were significantly more likely to be present in families of children excluded from school (early maternal separation and serious illness of parent) impacted on the children and their families. These stories are taken from interviews with the children as well as from those with their parents.

Early maternal separation

Half of the children in the excluded group had been separated from their mother for a period of at least four consecutive weeks between the ages of 6 months and 24 months. In two cases the children (Stephen, separated aged 6 months until 11 months and Kevin, separated aged 13 months until 3 years) lived with their respective maternal grandmothers due to poor housing and accommodation difficulties.

In the case of Stephen, his mother and her two other children were at first housed in bed and breakfast accommodation. Mother told us that she had been unable to cope with the baby there. Her mother offered to have Stephen but was not able to accommodate the rest of the family. Stephen's mother told me that she thought that it was 'better all round' that he stayed with her mother, who lived in a different part of the country, about 75 miles away. Stephen's mother and the other children visited usually at the weekends and eventually the family was reunited when they were rehoused five months later. Stephen's mother told us that she missed Stephen, but had felt less close to him when she visited and when he eventually came home. She felt that he had settled well with his grandmother (who has since died) and that he had never really felt like 'her baby'. Stephen told us about living with his grandmother although he said that he did not remember being there. He had always felt that he had a special relationship with his grandmother and had been upset when she had died (when he was about seven years old).

Kevin had also lived with his maternal grandmother and step-grandfather, whilst his mother, who had six older children, tried to get rehoused. The family had been living in a different local authority and were trying to be rehoused in the local authority where the mother's parents lived and where the mother herself had been brought up. Kevin and two of his older siblings moved to live with their grandparents, the two older siblings attending school and Kevin staying home with his grandmother. Kevin's mother told us that Kevin and her other children stayed with her parents for much longer than she had intended but she became pregnant again and was unable to have them back home. When she did eventually secure housing in the local authority of her choice she explained that Kevin had wanted to stay with his grandparents although the two other children were happy to return home. Kevin had cried for his grandmother and started to wet the bed. Mother explained that she had understood his distress and had thought about letting him stay with his grandparents on a permanent basis. However, the grandmother's husband had said that he did not want the children to stay, although mother felt that her mother would have agreed. Kevin's case is interesting in that it would seem that he experienced a double maternal separation – first from his natural mother, at the age of 13 months, and then from his grandmother, who had been his secure maternal carer, at the age of 3 years.

Five of the other excluded cases of early separation from mothers were a result of mothers being hospitalised. In the case of Peter, his mother was hospitalised from 14 weeks into a twin pregnancy, when Peter was 24 months old. Peter stayed at home with his father and a neighbour helped to take him to a day nursery. A family friend would stay with Peter whilst his father visited his mother in hospital. Peter was able to visit his mother occasionally at weekends, but mother told us that he was so clinging to her and cried so much when he left that she found it too upsetting and thought it was probably better if he did not visit. She said that she used to speak to him on the telephone but that his own speech was not very clear at that time and she found it difficult to communicate with him. Until her hospitalisation, Peter had been at home all the time with his mother and they had been very close. Mother told us that it was a very difficult time for them all, and she eventually lost one of the twins. The surviving twin, a girl, had to stay in hospital for three months after the birth and both parents had visited daily. They usually took Peter with them for these visits. Mother said that when her daughter eventually came home Peter started to miss nursery school, and she was torn between letting him take up his free place, and keeping him home to be with her and his sister. She felt that it was better that he went to nursery and he seemed to settle well.

Philip's mother spent the last two months of her pregnancy with Philip's sister in hospital. Philip, then aged 16 months, saw her each week and his paternal grandmother moved in to look after him and his older sister. Philip's father was working away from home but returned at the weekends when his mother would return to her home. Mother told us that she only learnt much later that during this time Philip started to wet the bed and had a night seizure. Father and his mother decided not to worry mother by telling her, and she learnt about it from her health visitor about a year later.

Simon and Terry were separated from their mothers from the ages of 13 months and 18 months respectively because of mother's illness. Simon's mother was clinically depressed and spent three months in a psychiatric hospital about ten miles from their home. She had suffered from post-natal depression following Simon's birth and had threatened suicide when Simon was about eight months old. She had received support as an outpatient but started to neglect Simon and she and her husband had asked their GP for more help. Mother came home from hospital at the weekends and father, who was unemployed, stayed at home to look after Simon. When we met with mother (now divorced) she told us that at the time she did not think that Simon was really affected by all this, but she never felt that he was close to her after that.

Terry's mother was hospitalised for two months following a serious car accident. Terry was not involved in the accident. Mother damaged her spine and was unsure if she would be permanently paralysed. She seems to have made a full recovery although she told us that she does experience bad pain from time to time. She was sent to a specialist spine injury hospital for treatment and saw Terry and his older brother at the weekends. She describes how difficult it was for her because the children wanted her to hold them and she was unable to move. She said that the children had not really understood and that although she had looked forward to seeing them the visits were very stressful. Mother explained that her sister had looked after the children as she was a single parent, and her parents had brought the children to the hospital. When she returned home she found the children were out of their usual routines and were difficult for her to manage.

Warren was 15 months old when his mother went into prison until he was four and a half years old. Warren lived with his maternal grandmother during this time. He was taken to see his mother for his birthday and at Christmas although mother told us that she had wanted to see him more often. When she came out of prison she had lived with Warren and her mother for about a year before she and Warren were able to move to their own flat nearby. Mother told us that she was able to get to know Warren again during the year following her release from prison. She said that he did know that she was his mother, and he had not thought that his grandmother was his mother. When they moved she explained that Warren, then aged about five and a half to six years, was able to stay at his school and he seemed happy. He continued to see his grandmother daily.

David was born in Jamaica and, when he was four months old, his mother travelled to the UK to join her husband, leaving David with his maternal grandmother in Jamaica. She travelled back to Jamaica once a year to see him and eventually he came to live with his parents in the UK when he was five years of age. Mother explained that it was important that she and her husband made a 'good' home for their family before they sent for David, and that they had wanted him to attend school in the UK. She also explained to us that this is not an uncommon situation for African-Caribbean families, and that grandmothers are seen as usually the best person to raise young children. She told us that David had just accepted the situation, and when we spoke with David he remembered his time in Jamaica with his grandmother as a happy time. He said that he was also happy to have moved to be with his parents in the UK. David told us that he does not remember missing his mother although he did look forward to her visits and always knew that one day he would go to the UK to be with her and his father.

Nicola was born when her mother was 15 years old, and she and her mother lived with the maternal grandmother. When Nicola was one year old her mother moved out and left Nicola with her grandmother. Mother returned for Nicola four years later, when she had married and had two more children. During her absence Nicola had seen her mother occasionally and had met her new husband and the two other children 'a few times'. Nicola told us that her grandmother had wanted her to stay but Nicola felt that her natural mother wanted her and she liked her new brother and sister. Nicola told us that her grandparents had later moved away and that she now sees them only occasionally.

John was separated from his mother when he was hospitalised for six weeks, aged 19 months old, having been injured in a road accident. He had run into the road outside his uncle's house, was hit by a car and taken to hospital for emergency treatment. His parents told us that John had been given a 50–50 chance of surviving the first night. He had a fractured skull, broken leg and broken ribs. John stayed in intensive care for a week and stayed in hospital for a further four weeks. His parents visited him every day although he was in a hospital near his uncle's home, some distance from the family home. After three weeks he was transferred nearer home. Mother explained that, as they have three other children, she was unable to stay in hospital with John, although she had wanted to. She or her husband saw him every day.

Of the comparison group only three pupils had experienced early separation from their mothers. Jane was separated from age 18 months to age 20 months, Tom from age 20 months to age 24 months, and Clive from age 18 months to age 21 months. In each case the separation was due to their mothers being hospitalised during difficult pregnancies. During the period of separation Jane lived at home with her father, where she and her two sisters were looked after by a live-in au pair. Tom and Clive were both cared for by maternal grandmothers who moved into the family home.

Particular differences between the two groups with regard to early separation from mother seem to be the reason for the separation, and the care arrangements during the separation. In each of the comparison cases the children were separated from their mothers due to hospitalisation during difficult pregnancies, and the mothers reported that they had some time to prepare for the hospitalisation, to prepare their children and to make adequate child-care arrangements. There seems to be little difference between the children in terms of by whom and where the children were cared for. Of the ten excluded pupils who were separated from their mothers, three mothers reported the separation as being sudden and unexpected. These were John who had the road accident, Terry whose mother was involved in a car accident and Warren whose mother was imprisoned. Warren's mother told us that she had not expected to be given a custodial sentence, and she had not made any care arrangements for Warren. She thought that, as a first offender and the mother of such a young child, she would be given probation. She told us that her main fear was that Warren would be taken into care and that she would never see him again. She said that she had shouted to her mother to take Warren but did not know until five days later that her mother had been allowed to look after him.

All of the comparison group children were looked after either by their father with help from an au pair or by maternal grandmother, in each case in their own homes. In the case of the excluded group, three of the children were looked after in their own homes by their father or maternal grandmother, one with help from a family friend.

The remaining children (with the obvious exception of John who was in hospital) were cared for by other family members outside their own home context.

Parents of the comparison children reported no visible consequences of the separation. Parents of the excluded children, in contrast, reported the start of bed-wetting in the case of two children, a change of routine and difficulties in managing behaviour in one case, night seizure in one case, being clinging and upset in another, and the development of a special relationship with the substitute carer in another case. In five of the ten excluded cases mothers reported no visible consequences of the separation.

Our data is thus consistent with findings from previous studies of early separation, and particularly hospitalisation (e.g. Stacey *et al*, 1970; Weiner *et al.* 1992) in that those children whose mothers reported noticing some adverse consequences of the early separation tended to have additional stress factors taking place. In cases in the excluded group where no adverse consequences were reported, the separation had either been relatively short (as in the case of Stephen for just five months) or had been for an extensive period of time but with a substantial degree of stability with the substitute carer (as in the case of Warren for four and a half years whilst his mother was in prison, David for five years whilst he had lived with his grandmother in Jamaica and Nicola for three years when she had lived with her grandmother in the house where she had lived all of her life). In the case of the five excluded pupils where adverse consequences were reported, the additional family stresses included poor housing and illness of mother, including one case of mental illness.

Serious illness of parent

The two cases (Simon and Terry) already mentioned where mother's illness resulted in maternal separation are included in the six children identified in the excluded group as having one parent suffering from a serious illness over the past five years. There were no such cases found in the comparison group. In four cases the family reported at least one family stressor in addition to the serious illness of one parent. In addition to the description of Simon and Terry's circumstances, they have both experienced stress from their mothers' chronic medical conditions from a very young age (from birth and from 18 months old respectively).

In the case of the four other children (Philip, Nicola, Gary, Warren) their parents' condition started when they were older. Philip and Nicola were at secondary school at the onset of their fathers' conditions and Gary and Warren were at primary school. It is interesting to note that both Philip and Nicola were permanently excluded from school within one year of their fathers being diagnosed with serious medical conditions. Both Warren and Gary's mothers reported violent behaviour as one impact of the fathers' condition, and both reported a history of marital conflict over an extended period of time, prior to diagnosis.

Results of family resilience assessment

The help of four experienced educational psychologists was enlisted to assess family resilience. All first met with the first author and discussed the eight themes. We then asked them to attend as they listened to the taped interviews. Discussion was designed to induce a measure of agreement as to what each theme implied, and what kinds of responses might indicate presence of a particular theme. Listeners were provided with record sheets upon which all the taped interviews could be rated for these eight themes in the discourse of the interview. We were interested not merely in the presence of a theme in the discourse, but also in the strength of its representation. The prepared record sheet therefore asked each listener not only to note the presence of each theme, but also to rate its strength, by marking a prepared line, 5 inches long, which represented a continuum from 'weak' (i.e. not present) to 'strong' (i.e. showing a strong presence). The distance from the left-hand end of each rating line to each listener's strength mark was measured and provided a percentage strength rating for each theme. Two listeners took each tape home and independently listened and recorded their rating of each theme.

Inter-rater reliability was assessed using a procedure based on work by Quattrone and Jones (1980) and Wilder (1984) examining homogeneity and perception of variability within groups. The first author listened to all the taped interviews, thus providing a basis of consistency. The four educational psychologists each listened to and rated ten taped interviews. Strength ratings for each theme in each interview were then compared across the pairs of listeners who had provided the ratings, in order to assess inter-rater reliability. Differences in ratings were analysed by t-tests. As no differences approached statistical significance, we concluded that there was satisfactory agreement across pairs. We should point out that listening to the tapes made it obvious to the listeners which parents were parents of excluded children and which were not: that is, blind rating was impossible.

The eight themes which listeners were asked to identify and rate are named and defined below. They represent our interpretation of factors found in previous studies to lead to resilience in children and their families (Antonovsky 1987; Jenkins and Smith 1990; Weiner *et al.* 1992; Hawley and De Haan 1996).

Theme 1: Coherence. Evidence that the family members are able to give a clear, comprehensible and chronological account of family events and history.

Theme 2: Positive reframing. Evidence that the family members can reframe negative events (risk factors) in a way which gives a positive outcome; for example, where divorce can be seen as something which has been ultimately beneficial.

Theme 3: Family flexibility. Evidence that the family can adapt to unexpected or unusual circumstances.

Theme 4: Comprehension (cognition) of events. Evidence that the family have a cognitive understanding of events (including an understanding of education structures and procedures, and the roles of professionals).

Theme 5: Description of child's easy temperament. Evidence of at least one parent describing the child as 'easy'; use of descriptions such as 'placid', 'quiet', 'a good sleeper/eater', 'no trouble' and 'a good baby'.

Theme 6: Well-defined social support. Evidence of non-professional support from outside the immediate family, including friends, neighbours, extended family.

Theme 7: Family routines. Evidence that family roles are stable (e.g. who cooks, shops, deals with education, child-care arrangements, payments of bills, etc.) and family routines are important (e.g. bed times, meal times, holidays, etc.).

Theme 8: Mother's enjoyment of own schooling. Evidence that the child's mother had a positive view of her own experience of school.

Mean strength ratings for each identified aspect of resilience (theme) are shown in Table 4.2. These data were analysed using Mann-Whitney tests. It is immediately apparent from Table 4.2 that families of the excluded group demonstrated lower resilience in all areas

Table 4.2 Strength ratings of aspects of resilience in families of excluded and control children

Theme	Mean strength of resilience in families			
	Excluded per cent	Comparison per cent	M-W z	p
Coherence	52.9	72.8	−3.2	<.001
Positive reframing	19.3	66.8	−7.2	<.0001
Family flexibility	26.4	67.8	−6.5	<.0001
Comprehension of events	35.1	85.7	−6.4	<.0001
Child's easy temperament	51.6	79.8	−4.9	<.0001
Social support	27.2	81.5	−6.4	<.0001
Family routines	37.2	76.5	−5.6	<.0001
Mother's enjoyment of schooling	26.3	90	−5.4	<.0001

assessed. Differences between the two groups for each theme are discussed below, illustrated with extracts from the taped interviews.

Coherence

Coherence was rated as one of the strongest resilience characteristics of families of the excluded group, with a mean resilience rating of 52.9 per cent. This was however weaker than coherence in the comparison families. The following extracts illustrate the difference between a high and low rating for coherence. The first extract shows the description of an event that contains a chronological sequence and a sense of shared understanding of events:

Mr and Mrs A (Robert, comparison) describing a family holiday when Robert was taken to hospital with a severe asthmatic attack

Mrs A: We were down in Torquay and it was hot . . .
Mr A: Yes, I remember it was really hot wasn't it – especially in the car – we were sweltering . . .
Mrs A: and we got to the caravan where we'd been before
Mr A: It belongs to a mate of mine at work . . .
Mrs A: Anyway Robert had been OK but in the night came through to us and he couldn't breathe . . .

Mr A: Poor kid – he was very bad and I knew we had to get him to hospital . . .

Mrs A: He'd used his spray but he was bad wasn't he?

Mr A: Yes, I got the car straight away and we took him . . . I didn't know if he was going to make it.

Mrs A: They were really good at the hospital and got him under control – it was a big scare.

Mrs B (Kevin, excluded) describing a similar incident when her son Kevin had a severe asthmatic attack:

Mrs B: When he was in hospital it was still scary . . . I went with him – I phoned um I think I phoned the doctor first and, or did I? Well anyway when we got to the hospital they rushed him in and a woman I know was there – I think she works there, or maybe she doesn't, I don't remember. He'd had attacks before and he's got his inhaler – it's here somewhere now – he should have it with him now but he hasn't. Anyway he'd woken up and I heard him struggling to breathe and his sister told me. I wasn't too worried 'cause he's had attacks before but it didn't get better. I think my daughter rang the doctor. He was in a state and my daughter rang for a taxi and they took us. Anyway this woman that I knew at the hospital her son is something at the school . . . they kept him in for the night and Mr T who knew him, saw him next day. It was worrying and he's had other attacks but not stayed in.

In the first extract Mr and Mrs A present a coherent account of Robert's attack, where and when it took place, who did what – Mr A 'got the car'. They agreed with the circumstances of events, such as 'it was hot' and 'we knew we had to get him to hospital'.

In the second extract Mrs B's account is less easy for the listener to follow. In her description of events she starts the story in the hospital after the attack, and then describes events at the house before the attack. She is unclear about who did what – 'I phoned the doctor first um or did I?' and later says that her daughter 'phoned the doctor'. She talks about a woman at the hospital but it is unclear who this woman is and how she is relevant to the story. Mrs B also talks about Mr T seeing Kevin. Eventually it became clear from further questioning that Mr T is the doctor at the hospital whom Kevin had seen as an outpatient. It never became clear who the woman was. Mrs B's accounts of other incidents and events, including Kevin's exclusion from school, were similarly described in a style that was difficult to follow, and which were presented out of the chronological sequence in which they took place. All listeners gave this style of description of events a low coherence rating.

Positive reframing

The families of excluded and comparison children also differed with respect to their ability to positively reframe negative events, to find something good. The following extracts demonstrate the difference in ability to find something positive in the outcome of a negative event.

Mr and Mrs C (comparison) describing the effect of the death of Mr C's father

Mr C: When my father died it was difficult wasn't it?

Mrs C: Yes, for all of us really 'cause my Mum was ill at the time and we needed to be there for his Mum and we were under a lot of strain really.

Mr C: Yes and I think it hit the kids 'cause they, well especially M, were close to his Nan and it upset her to see him so upset . . .

Mrs C: Yes, he used to stay with his Nan and they got even closer . . .

Mr C: I think we all got a bit closer after that 'cause we didn't see them a lot before but then we had my Mum over every Sunday for her dinner and we have Christmas together don't we – 'cause my Dad was a bit . . . Well, he liked to be quiet didn't he.

Ms D (excluded) describing the effect of her mother's death six years ago

Ms D: When my Mum died it was awful and I never got over it even now, what six years ago now, and it was sudden and since then I don't have anyone . . . the kids cry now and say they miss Gran – it's left a big hole which we'll never fill – she gave us a lot and now there's no one . . .

Family flexibility

Families of the excluded group also received significantly lower ratings for flexibility. The following extracts demonstrate differences between two families.

Mrs E (comparison) describing her response to her husband's redundancy

Mrs E: We knew it was on the cards so we could make some plans – like we tightened our belts and had to tell the children they couldn't go on school trips . . . he didn't get much pay-off 'cause there were so many of them laid off and he'd only been there what two years, a bit less I think. So I got a little job cleaning and we went on the social but we managed all right and he's got another job now, but you can get through can't you? You have to, as I say, tighten your belts and work together . . .

Ms F (excluded) describing her response to managing with her son's exclusion from school

Ms F: I have to work full time so there's no one to look after him in the day so he stays in and watches TV. I don't let him out but I think he goes out . . . I could come home for my dinner but it's a bus ride and he's OK at home. I can't do anything about it 'cause I have to work and anyway he should be at school not home . . . He gets himself some chips and eats me out of house and home . . . I still give him his dinner money so he uses that . . .

In the first extract Mrs E describes how the family was able to change some things in order to cope with the loss of income following Mr E's redundancy. Mrs E was able to get a job and the children were not able to go on school trips. There is evidence in the extract that the family was able to adapt to their new situation.

In the second extract Ms F gives no indication that she has been able to change from her usual routine of working full time and not returning home at 'dinner' time. It is unclear as to whether Ms F actually gets in extra food for her son Jack to eat during the day, although it seems that he leaves the house to buy chips with the money he would use for lunch if he were still attending school. There is no evidence in the interview of any flexibility in the family arrangements following Jack's exclusion. Again, this observation is not intended to be judgemental, but rather highlights that flexibility may be easier for some families than for others. Mrs E was fortunate to be able to get a job when her husband was made unemployed. Ms F was not able to give up work and may not have been able to reduce her hours when Jack was excluded from school.

Comprehension of events

The two extracts which follow, one from the text of an interview with a mother of an excluded pupil and one from an interview with the mother of a comparison pupil, demonstrate the difference between a low and high rating for comprehension of events.

Mrs G (comparison), Brian's mother, talking about her understanding of his educational needs

Mrs G: They told us that he had some reading problems and I knew that really and had been worried. So when the school said that they could get him some help from the tuition centre we thought that was a good idea. They explained about a statement and it seemed a good idea. It took a long time but we were kept informed and I knew that they're very busy. He got the help without the statement and he's fine now.

Mrs H (excluded) describing her understanding at the time of her son Philip's exclusion

Mrs H: I didn't know what they meant when they said he couldn't go back . . . it could have been for that day and I don't know how I was supposed to know . . . they said I could find another school and I said 'Where?' and they just talked like I knew what I should do . . . The centre said I could do something like appeal and sent me some stuff on it but it was all double Dutch to me . . . It all seemed a mess and we weren't told what was happening for ages . . .

The difference between these two extracts in terms of evidence of cognitive understanding lies in the use of phrases such as 'I don't know' and 'I didn't know' in Mrs H's extract, suggesting a lack of understanding compared with Mrs G who used the words 'I knew that really', 'they explained . . . and it seemed like a good idea' and 'I know they're very busy' suggesting an understanding of events. The examination of such language does not suppose a lack of intellectual ability on the part of those parents who appeared not to have an understanding of events. It is more an interpretation of how those parents process or are helped to process information at times of stress and worry.

Child's easy temperament

This was rated the second strongest resilience factor in families of excluded children, but still not as strong as in families of comparison children. The following extracts demonstrate the kinds of descriptions parents gave.

Ms I (control) describing her son Chris

Ms I: Chris was such a lovely little boy, he was always a good baby you know even when he was poorly – oh yea, he'd cry then but you'd give him a cuddle and he'd come up smiling . . . he'll still ask me for a cuddle now but not when anyone's around . . . We're lucky 'cause he's a good kid . . .

Mrs J (excluded) describing her son Adam

Mrs J: He was difficult when he was little . . . crying and that and we had a problem with his feeding like. My health visitor said she'd never heard anything like it his crying all the time. We had him checked out like but it was just the way he was . . . I never got any sleep 'til he was about two . . . he's always been – you know – demanding . . .

The first extract describes a child who smiled and liked (and still likes) cuddles. This description is of a child who would be easy to manage and easy to enjoy. The second extract describes a child who is demanding and stressful. He was a child who had difficulty feeding and sleeping which resulted in his mother not getting any sleep.

Worrying about such a baby and lack of sleep in itself is likely to result in a build-up of stress within the family.

Well-defined social support

There was the greatest mean difference between the two groups for well-defined social support, with a mean rating of 27.2 per cent for the excluded group and 81.5 per cent for the control group. This demonstrates the importance to family resilience of feeling supported during difficult times.

Ms K (comparison) describing her family support network

Ms K: We're really lucky 'cause we all grew up in a tight family, you know what I mean – my Nan and all that was always close by and popping in and out ... and if we've ever needed anything – not money like but help then I know just where I can go. I think the kids know that as well. We would never be short of help.

Mrs L (excluded) describing her support network

Mrs L: I never got any help about the exclusion, only what I could find out myself. But it's always been like that 'cause I've always had to do things for myself. I've got some friends and that but they can't really tell me what I want to know and they got kids of their own and their own troubles. I think you have to manage on your own and you can't rely on anyone else. That's what I tell my kids.

Family routines

Again, the families of excluded children received significantly lower ratings on this aspect of resilience. The following extracts demonstrate the presence of family roles and routines.

Mrs M (comparison) describing family routines

Mrs H: We always eat together as a family. I think that's important not with the TV on. We're lucky because we all get home about the same time, about 5 pm unless my husband gets held up but he's not on you know shift work, then the kids have to wash up. We don't have a machine and they grumble but they do it. My husband sometimes helps them with the pots. I cook . . .

Mrs N (excluded) describing family roles

Mrs N: I'm always the one who goes up to the school, you know, if there's any trouble or parents' evenings. It's me that does that. I've done it for all my children. My husband's not very good at that – it's not that he's not interested but he leaves it to me. He's more the one for sorting out the money you know. I leave all that to him.

In these two accounts both mothers are describing how their families organise their everyday domestic arrangements. Mrs M describes family routines, and Mrs N describes how the roles are organised in the family. In both cases these families were given a high rating for roles and routines. Those families that received a low rating for roles and routines presented more haphazard arrangements or were unable to recall or report who in the family was most likely to engage in particular tasks or take on particular responsibilities.

Mother's enjoyment of schooling

Fourteen of the nineteen mothers of the excluded group reported not having enjoyed their own schooldays. Of these, ten described how they had not been in any trouble at school but had not felt encouraged by their teachers to do well, and were eager to leave school as soon as possible. The other four mothers described having had difficulties at school, with one describing how she had missed a great deal of school as her own mother had allowed her to stay at home. Only two mothers of the comparison group described not having enjoyed school and being eager to leave as soon as possible.

Discussion of within-family results

Families of excluded children had experienced overall more risk factors than those of comparison children. This was particularly the case for early separation from mother, and serious illness of a parent. Excluded children were also more likely than comparison children to have experienced a large combination of different risk factors. Our research therefore agrees with previous findings of excessive exposure to stress in families of excluded children.

Families of excluded children also received consistently lower ratings than those of comparison children on factors that have been shown in previous research to contribute to unexpectedly good outcomes for children predicted on the basis of risk factors to be at risk of poor outcomes. This provides further support for Rutter's proposals that negative outcomes for such children are not inevitable but depend on the ways in which risk factors are mitigated by resilience.

In predicting outcomes, it is necessary to look at the whole family context, and to assess family strengths as well as problems. This is likely to be even more important in attempts to intervene to improve outcomes for individual children. Very little in the way of intervention was available to the excluded children in our study, and their families reported feeling very unsupported by official agencies during and following the exclusion process. Yet there were some strengths here that could have been built on even (or perhaps, most profitably) at this crisis point.

If one context (e.g. the home) proves to be particularly stressful for children, the presence of a parallel context (e.g. the school) providing stability and calmness may provide a sufficiently containing context in which the child can function with enough resilience to withstand the stressful events of the home, and vice versa. This had clearly not happened for the excluded children in our study, who experienced difficulties both at home and at school. Their school difficulties were perhaps compounded or even partially caused by intrapersonal characteristics such as low self-esteem and a tendency to be unable to accept personal responsibility for the outcomes of their behaviour, both of which were more pronounced in the excluded children than in their control peers.

Chapter 5

Understanding the schools
Co-operative or coercive ethos?

School is one of the key systems in a child's life, and the whole system of school is of great importance in relation to the context of school exclusion. There is a considerable bank of literature that supports the view that schools can and do make a difference, in both positive and negative ways, and that schools differ in how many children they exclude from school, in the reasons they give for permanent exclusions and in the manner by which they exclude pupils.

Schools can and do make a difference to their pupils

As recently as the mid-1970s most educational literature assumed that families were the major determinants of children's progress and educational outcomes, with schools able to make little difference (Bernstein 1971). Even when findings suggested that school could make a difference (e.g. Reynolds *et al.* 1976) professional, political and public discussion continued to focus upon family factors. McLean (1987) showed that disruption in schools was traditionally analysed at the individual child level, with the causes being generally located within the child and the child's family background and circumstances. However, more recent research into school effectiveness (Galloway *et al.* 1982; Mortimore *et al.* 1991, Reynolds and Cuttance 1992, Rutter and Giller 1983) has cast doubt on previously held assumptions of the impotence of schools, and raised professionals' awareness that it is no longer acceptable to use family background alone as a reason for educational failure. For example, Mortimore *et al.* (1988) interviewed children, teachers and parents, and tested the children's reading and mathematics performance. They reported that where there was progress in these areas, statistical analysis suggested that 25 per cent of progress made could be attributed to school factors and only 5 per cent to home factors. After three years, variations in pupils' progress in reading and mathematics owed more to school membership than to family background. In addition to academic outcomes, some studies (e.g. Tizzard and Hughes 1988) have explored children's feelings about school, discovering that, irrespective of socio-economic circumstances, catchment areas and family backgrounds, different schools engendered different feelings of liking or disliking school. Their work showed that schools differ in their effectiveness in different domains, so that social outcomes of schooling, such as whether or not pupils actually like school, are partially independent of academic outcomes.

Sylva (1994) reported that schools have direct effects upon children's educational achievement, and upon social cognitions and feelings. She claims that these effects may be just as powerful in predicting later outcomes as intelligence and school curriculum. Such indirect effects of school are more elusive because they are mediated by children's motivation to learn, or motivation to avoid learning, by their conception of themselves as pupils and learners, and by the attributions they create for explaining success and failure.

School ethos and school effectiveness

Rutter *et al.* (1979) suggested that the most important factor in both academic and behavioural achievement among pupils is 'school ethos'. In their study, *Fifteen Thousand Hours*, Rutter *et al.* looked at the effect of 39 process variables in twelve Inner London schools. The most important aspect of this work was the analysis of the effects of the *combinations* of the variables, implicitly adopting a systemic approach. The fact that the combined effect of all process measures was much more powerful than that of any individual factor considered on its own led Rutter *et al.* to propose a community identity factor, 'an ethos', which had a greater influence upon pupil outcomes than any individual school process variables. They considered the following three variables were important in this 'institutional effect':

1   *Values*: which are inherent in teacher expectation of standards, models provided by teachers, and feedback received by pupils.
2   *Consistency*: described as 'the atmosphere of any particular school will be greatly influenced by the degree to which it functions as a coherent whole, with agreed ways of doing things

which are consistent throughout the school and have the general support of all staff'.

3   *Level of pupil acceptance*: which influences the degree to which pupils share the education perspective, their own positions of responsibility within the school system, and the general atmosphere of co-operation and sharing between staff and pupils.

School ethos can be an elusive concept to pin down. The term is used to describe the values and attitudes that underpin the social organisation of the school. It is experienced as the overall tone, social climate and atmosphere of the school and exemplified in the quality of interaction between teachers and pupils, in teachers' approaches to pupil management and in the degree of care and attention that is given to the maintenance and appearance of buildings and classrooms. Of central importance are the social and physical conditions that are experienced by the pupils. Positive school ethos has been described by Cooper *et al.* (1994) as being associated with co-operative relationships and purposeful joint planning activities among staff, and a shared commitment among staff and pupils to positive educational and institutional values and goals. The implication is that in effective schools pupils have a powerful sense of their own self-worth and potential for achievement, which is fostered by positive staff attitudes and behaviour. There is a clear link here between school ethos and children's development of self-esteem and locus of control to which we have referred earlier in this book.

Measor and Woods (1984) hold the view that 'school ethos' would seem much more to be a moving set of relationships within which different groups and individuals are constantly in negotiation. Their work led them to conceptualise the ethos of a school as the 'middle ground', where teachers sought to make links with pupil cultures by appropriating elements of these that promised to further the school's aims. Conceptualising this as 'middle ground' has the advantage of recognising the existence of powerful and prior cultures and sub-cultures within the school, based upon, for example, ethnic, social class and gender differences. It also recognises the contrasting value systems and needs of individuals who differ in personality, abilities and resources. In systemic terms, this involves remaining aware of the operation and importance of different systems, whilst drawing clear boundaries between them.

Measor and Woods devote a considerable section of their study to a consideration of the employment of humour as an important factor in school ethos. When used by teachers and pupils together, humour helps to create a bond between the two. Its use allows teachers to defuse potentially explosive incidents. It is seen to aid discipline and allow control to be exercised in a way that emphasises the bonds between pupil and teacher whilst at the same time informing the pupils that they are behaving inappropriately. Humour can provide the pupil with status whilst at the same time allowing the teacher to exercise control in a way acceptable to the pupil. In systemic terms 'punctuation' will also play a part here. An authority figure entering a classroom and overhearing a child seemingly being rude to a teacher (especially if that child has already got a 'bad name' in school) may immediately reprimand the pupil, without discovering the innocent events which led up to the apparent rudeness, or that it was actually a piece of acceptable banter between teacher and pupil.

Other findings, reported by Reynolds (1996), propose leadership, high expectations of pupils, parental involvement, pupil involvement, staff cohesion and consistent experiences for pupils as being central factors for effective schools. Reynolds and Sullivan (1979, 1981) studied school effectiveness in eight comprehensive schools. They collected data on school rules, resources and organisation in an attempt to learn more about what happens within individual schools that dramatically affects the social and academic development of the pupils. They also investigated the methods and beliefs of the head teachers and staff, and the system of rewards and punishments used. They reported that few teachers, academics or educationalists at that time believed that schools in themselves could do much to resist social disadvantage or turn educational failures into educational successes. The emphasis was on a 'cycle of deprivation' explanation, whereby schools faced with children who were vulnerable to educational disadvantage and failure because of deprivation in their home background were powerless to facilitate change.

Despite the professionals' belief in powerlessness, Reynolds and Sullivan found differences in ethos between more and less effective schools. More effective schools were characterised by an ethos of 'incorporation', whilst the least effective schools displayed an ethos of 'coercion'. The staff in the coercive schools held negative attitudes towards their pupils, seeing them as being in need of containment, control and character training. They employed deficiency explanations for the high levels of learning and behavioural difficulties they observed in their pupils. Teaching and management strategies that were associated with this view tended towards the punitive and confrontational; staff–pupil relationships were, by and large, of an impersonal nature. The incorporative ethos, however, was characterised by the teachers' positive view of pupils and their parents, by recognition of the essential worth and individuality of each child, and by a commitment to the aim of eliciting the voluntary involvement of the pupils and parents in school life. Teaching and management strategies associated with incorporative schools emphasised pupil responsibility, self-discipline, and involvement in lessons and in the wider life of school. Staff–pupil relationships tended to be marked by interpersonal rather than impersonal styles, with the emphasis on mutual respect and partnership. Learning and behavioural problems tended to be approached in a therapeutic manner, with the emphasis being on the pupil's need for support. There are clear links here to the development of locus of control (development of pupil responsibility and self-discipline) and self-esteem (relationships based in mutual respect and partnership).

In many ways Reynolds and Sullivan tend to see patterns of school organisation as being determined by staff attitudes. It is probably more accurate to think of the relationship between attitudes and organisation as interactional rather than unidirectional. It is reasonable to hypothesise, on the basis of research into teacher and pupil perspectives on classroom disruption, that teachers in coercive schools see the behaviour and attainments of their pupils as justification for their negative attitudes, and that disruptive pupils in such schools often feel that their negative behaviour is a justifiable response to coercive treatment. In incorporative schools a similarly self-fulfilling but opposite prophecy may be at work. Pupils are subject to the influences of the prevailing culture of the school (as presumably are teachers), adopting modes of adaptation to the institution which serve to perpetuate the prevailing culture, whether or not this is beneficial to all, or any, of the participants in the school organisation. All the aforementioned characteristics of effective schools suggest a commitment to the pupil as an active and valued participant in school life, and imply an image of the pupil as one of a group of worthy individuals, in need of care, consideration and nurture.

McManus (1987) describes two different types of approach to behaviour that he calls 'harmonised' and 'synchronised'. Harmonised schools tend to have few rules and fewer offences resulting in exclusions. Power and responsibility is shared between teachers and pupils, management of unacceptable behaviour is seen as included in the teacher's professional responsibilities, and head teachers are not normally referred to for discipline intervention in the first instance. Synchronised schools will take the opposite view. There will be clear rules as to which behaviours will result in exclusion, with a reluctance to make exceptions. Managing unacceptable behaviour is seen as an impediment to the teacher's proper task of teaching. These two extremes mirror the descriptions of the 'incorporative' and 'coercive' schools as described by Reynolds and Sullivan (1979), and the descriptions of a social democratic and humanist or a classical controlling approach to education as suggested by Parsons (1999).

Between-school differences in rates of exclusion

It is well established that some schools exclude more than others (Galloway *et al.* 1982). In addition, not only do exclusion rates differ greatly from school to school in a way that has little to do with the incidence of disruptive behaviour, but there are interesting and consistent differences in relation to the time of year, with twice as many exclusions in winter as in summer, and peaks in the middle of a term. Galloway *et al.* (1982) had similar findings, showing that exclusions peaked in November and again in February and March (the middle of the spring term). It is tempting to relate this seasonal variation to the different feelings engendered in us all by the short, dark, cold days of winter (when we feel tired and miserable) and the longer, light and at least occasionally sunny and warm days of summer (when we feel more optimistic and lively). It is also unsurprising that exclusions tend to peak in the middle of term, when teachers' energy and enthusiasm may be at their lowest ebb. Galloway *et al.* also reported that schools with the highest number of excluded pupils had the highest number of referrals of pupils with special educational needs, a statistic that echoes those reported in DfEE national statistics.

Imich (1994, 1995) reports that in one large county LEA in 1993–4, 24 per cent of all schools accounted for 75 per cent of all exclusions. His longitudinal study found no correlation between school exclusions and size of school or GCSE pass rates, although statistics collected by the DfEE show some evidence that school exclusion rates are negatively correlated with success rates at GCSE. Hayden (1997) also found that schools varied considerably in the numbers of pupils whom they excluded. The Secondary Heads' Association has suggested these differences can largely be explained by differences in school intake and catchment areas, but the Elton Committee (1989) concluded that the variation between schools is too great to be totally explained by catchment area alone, and others have suggested that the reasons are more complex than this. For example, Galloway *et al.* (1982) found no predictive relationship between easily measurable aspects of schools such as catchment area, levels of free school meals or school size, and levels of persistent absenteeism or exclusion from school. However, schools which had well-developed form teacher systems tended to have lower rates of disruptive behaviour. Galloway concludes that an understanding of the factors involved in exclusion requires intensive study of the individual school. It seems that differences in school ethos contribute not just to differences in school effectiveness, but also to differences in attitudes to and use of exclusion.

McManus (1987) also investigated the relationship between school catchment area and exclusion figures. His main findings were that school-related factors were the principal influence on the number of pupils a school suspends (excludes). There was no support for the view that high exclusion rates reflected deprived catchment areas. There was also no support for the view that children's problems in school are also present in the child's home. McManus (1989) argues that a school's declared policies and other written documents, including rules, are imperfect indicators of attitudes towards challenging behaviour, since schools do not always act in accordance with their public policies. McManus proposes that a school's rate of permanent exclusions may be taken as a more reliable indicator of its true threshold of tolerance. He concluded that, with the exception of vastly different social areas, the prevalence of socio-economic disadvantage of the intake of any school is not a reliable predictor of the exclusion rate of that school. The processes within the school appear to be more important in determining whether certain behaviours will result in exclusion from school. Where exclusion is used parents generally found the exclusion to be unhelpful, thus emphasising a breakdown of relationships between the school and parents. This was confirmed in a study carried out by the Rowntree Foundation (Parsons 1994), in which parents reported feeling very upset, shocked and devastated by their child's exclusion. For the most part they felt they had to fight hard for their child's return to school, and received little direct help in this. This has been a recurring theme in our interviews with parents of excluded children in our study, as will be shown in Chapter 6.

Factors which contribute to differential rates of exclusion

There have been conflicting findings with regard to relations between certain aspects of school ethos and effective behaviour control. Whereas Reynolds and Sullivan (1979) found that the most effective schools used therapeutic rather than punitive responses to misbehaviour, Rutter *et al.* (1979) found that the most effective schools employed disciplinary rather than therapeutic responses to similar presenting behaviours. Rutter suggested that tightly structured school organisations, which exert a high degree of institutional control over children, were more effective. Reynolds and Sullivan, however, found these tighter controlling policies were more associated with ineffective schools. Galloway (1985) says that no system per se can claim to be more effective than any other system, but that it is the commitment of the staff involved in implementing the chosen system which determines its effectiveness. In his study of four local head teachers whose schools had exceptionally low rates of disruptive behaviours, two were autocratic in style, one was democratic and the other was a combination of the two. The important determining factor was that all of these head teachers were successful in gaining the support of their staff for their philosophies and practices.

Coulby and Harper (1985) describe aspects of school organisation that can be linked to pupil behaviour. Their list includes rules and the way in which rules are applied; timetabling and practical arrangements for pupils moving around the school; teachers' responsibilities for each other and for their pupils; communication arrangements within the school; teacher–parent contact and attitudes; and provision of in-service training for teachers. They write extensively about the place and function of school rules, identifying the 'formal' and 'informal' rules of the organisation. They refer to the fact that it often takes a long time for a new member (pupil or teacher) of the organisation (school) to find out what the rules are. Coulby and Harper's view is that the function of rules is not to demand blind obedience from children but rather to encourage them to develop qualities of self-discipline and co-operation. They consider that this is more likely to be achieved if the rules are clear, understood, discussed and endorsed by all, rather than where a long list of largely unnecessary restrictions is produced by teachers, and subsequently enforced unquestioningly with an expectation of unquestioning obedience. Those schools which have taken seriously these aspects of behaviour management are most likely to be able to contain pupils with challenging behaviour, a fact which is likely to be reflected in their exclusion numbers.

McLean (1987) described the low excluding schools in his study as being more child focused, with the idea of exclusion from school being incompatible with their philosophy and ethos. Such schools were described as having fundamental principles of respect for the individual and forgiveness which made it inappropriate to 'reject' pupils and pass on responsibility for their education to someone else. Exclusion was seen as rarely solving problems. It was seen as inconsistent with the school's social responsibilities to put the pupils with problems out into the community where, with no supervision, they could possibly cause further difficulties, and certainly where they were unlikely to receive remediating help and support. Such schools operated flexible discipline systems and a positive proactive style of pupil management, taking an incorporative approach. These low excluding schools tended to embrace school discipline as a whole school responsibility by a generally united staff. The systems were reviewed and adapted in response to experience and the changing demands and circumstances of the organisation. The roles of class tutors and heads of pastoral care/department were of central importance, with the latter only becoming involved in matters of discipline if necessary at a later stage. Communication between class tutors, heads of pastoral care and department, and more senior management ensured that it was rare for senior members of staff to have to become involved with a pupil for a disciplinary reason without knowing a good deal about the background to the problem and what interventions had already been tried.

Parsons and Howlett (1995) explored ways by which pupils vulnerable to exclusion can be maintained in schools. One difficulty identified by schools was the recognition that, as order and discipline significantly contribute to the processes of learning and pupils' overall academic performance and examination success, it was essential that schools protected order and discipline. They would therefore eliminate any pupil who threatened order and discipline. Similarly, the many elements that comprise the ethos of the school can perpetuate and even create the aggression a school seeks to control. The introduction of league tables and published examination results and the encouragement for schools to enter the competitive marketplace will all have influenced teachers' attitudes to their roles, and consequently their attitudes to their pupils. Stirling (1991: 8) suggests that 'given open enrolment, the school with a number of these [disruptive] pupils or with a reputation for working with those pupils with high visibility – is likely to lose out in the pupil competition, particularly if they are in competition with grant maintained schools or city technology colleges'.

Badger (1985) writes that all secondary schools experience difficulty at some time in coping with the behaviour of a small minority of their pupils. The number of such pupils varies considerably from school to school, both because of the varying catchment areas between schools and because of the varying perceptions of and responses to disruptive behaviour between schools. Badger argues that difficult behaviour at secondary school can be 'traced back' through the primary school that the child attended, and 'indeed beyond'. Badger understands there to be an assumption (from primary and secondary school teachers) that behavioural characteristics are fixed. However, Badger's study demonstrated that it was mainly the *boys* identified as having behaviour problems at secondary school who were also remembered by their primary school teachers as having behaviour problems. This was not the case for girls. Overall 50 per cent of the pupils seen by secondary staff to be major disruptive influences were remembered as such by primary school staff, leaving 50 per cent who were not remembered as being disruptive or troublesome.

The school factors in the study

Galloway *et al.* (1982) report that a pupil's chances of being excluded are influenced as much, and probably more, by which school they happen to attend, as by any stress in their family or by any constitutional factors in the pupils themselves. By taking a systemic view, we hope to show that it is not even as simple as this. Schools do differ considerably in how they respond and relate to their pupils, but school is one part of a complex network of systems to which the child belongs, and addressing only what happens in schools is unlikely to address the needs of those pupils who, for whatever reason, find difficulty in responding in socially acceptable ways to authority, rules, discipline, stressful events, and in expressing and articulating their views and needs. We set out to identify the differences which schools can and do make, but in relation to the interrelationships of the child's other systems.

The schools used in the study were not specifically selected on the basis of high, medium or low exclusion rates, although these data were available. They were included solely on the basis of being the schools from which the randomly selected excluded group had been excluded. Therefore the pupils were selected in the first instance, and then the head teachers of the schools were approached to request their involvement. None of the schools approached refused to be involved in the study. The comparison group needed to be matched for school so were inevitably selected from the already participating schools.

On the basis of the literature review presented above, we expected to find differences in ethos between schools, and that these differences would influence how pupils with challenging behaviours were managed. It was also likely that the excluded pupils would describe their schools less positively than the control pupils. It was expected that the lowest excluding schools would be more likely to present an 'incorporative' ethos, and the highest excluding schools to present a 'coercive' school ethos (as described by Reynolds and Sullivan 1981).

Methods: Interviews

We planned to interview the head teachers of the ten schools attended by the comparison pupils (and from which the excluded pupils had been excluded), using a semi-structured interview schedule that explored recollections of events leading to the exclusion of the particular pupils of the study, (including any comments which the head teachers wanted to make in hindsight), school rules, and behaviour management issues. These interviews were taped and analysed according to the following themes.

What is the function of rules?

Responses here could be expressed in terms of control, or protection and safety of others, or the promotion of good conditions for learning, or to promote a sense of responsibility, or to facilitate living and working together.

1 *How and by whom are rules agreed?* Which members of the school community are involved in setting and agreeing rules: governors, head teachers, senior staff, all staff, pupils, parents – who is included?

2 *Have rules changed?* Society changes over time, and societal

changes impact on schools: to what extent have rules changed as a consequence of these external influences?

3 *How are rules communicated?* Responses here could include, by word of mouth, in written form, by example, by osmosis, regularly, intermittently.

4 *Are rules consistent?* Does the school consider consistency to be desirable and if so how is it achieved?

5 *Is there a place for idiosyncratic rules?* Are individual teachers allowed to introduce their own supplementary rules in addition to the basic school rules, and under what conditions are these idiosyncratic rules encouraged or tolerated?

6 *What are the basic ground rules?* Are there rules which apply all the time and to everyone?

7 *Which rules are most difficult to enforce?*

8 *How does the school respond to parental pressure to exclude?* Are parents able to influence decisions about exclusions, and do they?

9 *Are there set criteria for fixed term exclusions?*

10 *Is there a set criterion for length of exclusion?*

11 *Are there agreed arrangements for pupils returning to school?*

12 *Is there a set criterion for permanent exclusions or is the decision taken depending upon individual circumstances* (and if so, what might those be?).

Methods: Questionnaires

Six teachers with a different range of experience, roles and status (head teacher, deputy head teacher, head of learning support, newly qualified first year teacher, main scale teacher with minimum of three years experience, and head of year with pastoral responsibility) from each of the ten schools were then asked by their head teacher to complete a Teachers' School Ethos Questionnaire. Heads were free to select teachers within the required specifications. The parents of children in the excluded and comparison groups were asked to complete a Parents' School Ethos Questionnaire. The excluded and comparison pupils were asked to complete a Pupils' School Ethos Questionnaire.

The twelve indicators of school ethos investigated in these questionnaires were taken from the Scottish Office Education Department (1992) publication *Using Ethos Indicators in Primary School Self-Evaluation* and adapted slightly for use in English secondary schools. They are identical to the key dimensions identified by OFSTED (1995/6) as differentiating between effective and less effective schools.

1 *Pupil morale*: the degree to which pupils enjoy school and feel that what they are learning is interesting and relevant.

2 *Teacher morale*: the degree to which teachers feel that they receive support and recognition from colleagues, senior management and parents.

3 *Teachers' job satisfaction*: the degree to which teachers value teaching as a profession and feel that they are doing a worthwhile job.

4 *The physical environment*: the degree to which the school is seen as a safe, comfortable and pleasant environment for work and for leisure.

5 *The learning context*: the degree to which the classroom is seen as a stimulating working context and classroom learning is seen as satisfying and productive.

6 *Teacher–pupil relationships*: the degree to which harmonious relationships exist between teachers and pupils and whether or not they treat one another with courtesy and respect.

7 *Equality and justice*: the degree to which there are policies that are agreed upon and understood by staff and reflected in their day-to-day practice.

8 *Extra-curricular activities*: the degree to which opportunities are provided for learning and social activity outside the classroom, and seen as enjoyable and beneficial by pupils and teachers.

9 *School leadership*: the degree to which the head teacher and the senior management team provide inspiration, direction and support.

10 *Discipline*: the degree to which the school provides an ordered environment in which teachers feel able to teach and pupils feel able to work without interruption or intimidation.

11 *Information to parents*: the degree to which the school provides effective channels for communication between school and parents.

12 *Parent/teacher consultation*: the degree to which the school provides opportunities for exchange of information relevant to a particular pupil between parents and school.

Questionnaire returns

No questionnaires were returned by any of the staff from the two schools which had permanently excluded the highest numbers of children during the year in which children were recruited into our study. The governors of one of these schools had instructed the head teacher not to take any further part in the study. We were not given any reason for this decision, which was communicated to us by the head teacher. Examination of teacher questionnaire returns by school and teacher status showed that heads of year were least likely to respond, followed by heads of learning support. We had not predicted the low response from heads of year, as it had been assumed that they, in particular, would be involved in the very early stages of pupil behaviour which led to permanent exclusion, and that they might therefore have been particularly interested in participating in the study. The low response from heads of learning support may be explained by the small number who had been directly involved with those pupils who became excluded, as already discussed described in detail earlier. The overall rate of teacher questionnaire returns was 68 per cent (41 returns from 60 sent). This contrasts with the 100 per cent rate of return for parent and child questionnaires, which were administered during parental and child interviews.

Analysis of pupil questionnaires

The excluded and comparison groups' views of their schools were very similar in terms of how they rated the physical environment, the provision of extra-curricular activities, and the levels of pupil morale and of equality and justice, with no significant between-group differences when these ratings were analysed using Mann-Whitney tests. All pupils had generally positive views of the physical environment, the extra-curricular provision and pupil morale, and quite negative views of equality and justice. This negativity in respect of equality and justice indicates that all pupils tended to feel that policies were not agreed upon and understood by all staff, nor were they reflected in teachers' day-to-day practice. The fact that comparison pupils were equally as negative as the excluded with respect to ratings of equality and justice tempts us to interpret this negativity as an honest reflection of the reality of the school situation, rather than as sour grapes on the part of excluded pupils who, as our interview data show, tended to feel their exclusion from school had been unfair or unjustified. This interpretation is also supported from our interviews with head teachers, most of whom admitted that it was very difficult to ensure consistency of approach throughout the school.

The excluded group were significantly less positive than the comparison group about other aspects of school. The largest difference was in perceptions of teacher–pupil relations, with excluded pupils less likely to enthusiastically support the view that teachers were good, kind or sensitive to pupils' feelings. Interestingly, they were also more likely to feel negative about their teachers' likely job satisfaction, perhaps suggesting empathy with teachers' frustrations, possibly in respect of managing challenging behaviour as presented by the excluded pupils. There is certainly no suggestion in our data that the excluded group think teachers gain any satisfaction from excluding disruptive pupils. As we have already shown that the excluded group had more learning difficulties than the comparison, it is not surprising that they held more negative views of the learning context of the school, in terms of the kinds of support offered to those experiencing difficulty. Given the excluded group's higher degree of externality in terms of locus of control, it is also not surprising that they see the school environment as less ordered and disciplined than the comparison group. This allows them to ascribe their failure to adapt their behaviour to the school's requirements, which eventually resulted in their permanent exclusion, to the school's own failure to provide an ordered environment that facilitates high quality learning experiences and good social relationships.

Analysis of parent questionnaires

The only area in which parents of excluded pupils rated school equally as positively as parents of comparison pupils was in terms of the physical environment, with both groups rating this very positively. Parents of comparison pupils were generally positive about all other aspects of school, whereas the only other overall positive rating given by parents of excluded pupils was to approve the provision of information to parents, albeit significantly less positively than parents of comparison pupils. It is interesting here to consider the kinds of questions asked that underlie these data: the section of our parental questionnaire relating to 'information to parents' contains only questions that probe the one-way flow of information from school to parents. It is possible that had two-way communication or sharing of information between school and parents been probed, the parents of excluded children (or, indeed, of both groups) might have been generally less positive. This speculation gains some support from our interview data, where parents' and schools' accounts of the exclusion were frequently in disagreement as to the cause (and also often disagreed with the child's account), suggesting that no shared meaning of the event had been jointly constructed. These different accounts are presented and discussed in detail in Chapter 6.

Parents of excluded children were significantly more negative than comparison parents in rating all other aspects of school ethos, with their most negative rating reserved for equality and justice (also rated highly negatively by their children). It is perhaps likely that the significantly more negative view of school shown by parents of the excluded pupils was due to difficulty in dissociating their views of the school from the experience of their child's exclusion. However, had they considered that the school had provided adequately for their child's needs in any way, it should have been possible for these parents, even with the exclusion in mind, to have given a positive view of school life. It should also be noted that in some cases the parents had another child attending the school who had not been excluded.

Analysis of teacher questionnaires

It should be borne in mind during discussion of teacher questionnaire data that we had no data from the two schools that had excluded the most children (numerically, but not necessarily in proportion to school size) in the previous school year, and that, therefore, where we talk about high and low excluding schools, this is from a truncated range, and the two schools described hereafter as the highest excluding are in fact third and fourth highest among all twelve schools.

We first created a mean rating for each school ethos indicator from the combined responses of all respondents in each school, regardless of their role or status within the school. Comparison of these mean ratings showed that teachers in the two highest excluding schools (with four and five permanent exclusions) held more negative views of school ethos compared with teachers in the two lowest excluding schools (with one permanent exclusion each). However, all mean ratings were generally more positive than negative: that is, as a whole, teaching staff tended to view their school's ethos in positive terms.

We examined this further by re-analysing the data according to teacher status within the school, and comparing views of the two lowest status groups (newly qualified and main scale teachers) with those of the two highest status groups (head teacher and deputy head teacher). The lowest status group (16 responses) were significantly more negative than the highest status group (15 responses) with respect to nine of the twelve school ethos indicators (pupil morale, physical environment, learning context, teacher–pupil relations, equality and justice, school leadership, discipline, information to parents, and parent–teacher consultation). The highest status group were significantly more negative than the lowest status group in respect of the three remaining indicators (teacher morale, teacher job satisfaction, and extra-curricular activities).

These differences can perhaps be explained in terms of the different positions and day-to-day responsibilities and experiences of teachers within each status group. Those characteristics described more negatively by the lower status teachers are concerned with the more 'hands on' activities of school life – involving direct contact with pupils, parents, the material aspects of the school (such as the physical environment) and their experience of the prime task of the higher status teachers (school leadership). The three indicators rated more negatively by the high status group are concerned with those aspects of school life that perhaps relate more directly to personal as well as professional life. For example, provision of extra-curricular activities can intrude into personal life space and possibly nowadays provokes increasing anxiety in those professionals with most responsibility for its provision, given recent prosecutions of teachers following serious accident and injury to pupils on field trips. More negative ratings of teacher job satisfaction and teacher morale by the high status group might be attributed in part to this group's feelings of responsibility for more junior teachers' job satisfaction and morale, with their perceptions of this influenced by the complaints about aspects of their work that teachers are likely to bring to them, as well as by their own feelings of having increasingly too much to do. However, again, we need to emphasise that *more negative* does not equate here with *negative*: overall, the mean ratings of both groups tended to indicate a generally positive view of their schools, and in this respect were similar to those of the parents of comparison children.

Analysis of interviews with head teachers

Interviews were completed with all ten head teachers. When analysing these interviews, we were interested to examine the language used in responses to our questions in relation to Reynolds and Sullivan's descriptions of incorporate and coercive schools. These data are summarised in Table 5.1 in terms of the themes identified earlier; we then discuss each theme in more detail.

Table 5.1 Head teachers' responses in semi-structured interviews, by themes

School	1 = highest excluding 9 = lowest excluding	Function of rules	How rules are made	Rule changes, new rules	Communication of rules	Ensuring consistency	Idiosyncratic rules	Basic ground rules
1	4	To keep order and control the children	Staff	Uniform	Rules are displayed around the school	Not possible with 80 staff	Inevitable	No fighting, smoking, drugs
2	5=	For a shared understanding	Staff, head teacher	Re fashion	In school handbook	Difficult	Subject related	Safety for others
3	1=	To control for fair play	Staff	New rules all the time	Given school handbook on entering school	Not difficult if staff enforce rules properly	Not acceptable but happens a lot	No drugs, no smoking, no fighting
4	5=	We've always had them	Head, governors	Drugs	Regular reminders by staff	Impossible	Difficult for heads of year	Safety of others
5	8	For us all to know how to behave sensibly	School council, parents, head teacher	Hair styles and jewellery	Regular reminders, assemblies	Very difficult/ children have to work it out	Does exist but pupils have to learn about difference	Attention to work, safety of others

6	5=	For children to learn about working and living together	Staff, PTA	Drugs, uniform	Regular reminders	Very difficult	Inevitable but can cause problems	Safety for staff and pupils
7	1=	To control, a measure of authority	Senior staff, governors	No drugs, no knives	In handbook	All staff expected to enforce rules	Inevitable, children have to learn	No drugs, no knives and no violence
8	9=	To help provide a positive learning setting	Staff, parents, pupils	Drug	Regular reminders, classroom display	Impossible	Inevitable	Respect for others
9	9=	For civilised living as a learning community	Staff, parents, school council	Uniform, e.g. no trainers	Regular reminders, school handbook, minutes of council meetings	Very difficult, regular reminders to staff	Inevitable and acceptable to a point and often subject related	Respect for others' learning, safety of others
10	3	To avoid chaos, to keep order, so that parents know what we expect	Staff, governors	No knives, no alcohol	In handbook, updated each year	Difficult with weak teachers or NQTs	Does happen but to be discouraged	Punctuality and safety of others

Continued

Table 5.1 continued

School	Rank order re exclusions	Most difficult rules to enforce	Pressure from other parents to exclude	Criteria for fixed term exclusions	Usual length of fixed term exclusion	Arrangements on return from exclusion	Criteria for permanent exclusion
1	4	Uniform, smoking	Parents' views are important	Persistent minor offences	According to severity of incident	Straight back into class	Violence
2	5=	Smoking, uniform	Parents can make representation but do not dictate final decisions	Persistent mis-behaviour, isolated serious incident	Depends on the circumstance	Meeting with HOY and parents and pupil	Serious violence against adults or other pupils
3	1=	Smoking, uniform, fighting	Other parents' views can sway a decision for the good of the reputation of the school	First offence for smoking or fighting, not turning up for detention, truanting	Until parents come into school/depends upon severity of crime	Meeting with parents and head and pupil re final warning	Persistently not producing satisfactory work, persistent truanting, fighting

4	5=	Uniform	Taken into account	Persistent bad behaviour	Usually five days unless more serious	Meeting with HOY	Constant disruption of other pupils
5	8	Uniform	Decision always lies with the head	After two consecutive poor weekly reports	Usually for no more than three days	Meeting with parents and head and pupil	Very serious incident (unlikely to be isolated)
6	5=	Uniform, smoking	Head not swayed by other parents' views	Persistent poor behaviour	Depends on when parents can come into school	Meeting with parents and head and pupil	Violence to adult or pupil
7	1=	Smoking, uniform	Other children must be considered and their parents views are important	For failing to attend detention, fighting, two demerits for uniform deviance	Depends upon severity of crime, can be five days or fifteen days	Final warning meeting with parents and pupil	Bringing drugs or knives into school any violence
8	9=	Uniform	Head makes decision, not parents	When other sanctions have made no difference	Never more than two days unless pending permanent	HOY and school counsellor to set a programme	Serious act of violence

Continued

Table 5.1 continued

School	Rank order re exclusions	Most difficult rules to enforce	Pressure from other parents to exclude	Criteria for fixed term exclusions	Usual length of fixed term exclusion	Arrangements on return from exclusion	Criteria for permanent exclusion
9	9=	Uniform	Other parents don't usually know full facts	Through discussion with parents, for a cooling off period	Depends upon reason but usually no more than three days	Straight back into class, parents to meet head	Severe attack on pupil or adult
10	3	Smoking, uniform	Parents can sway a decision	Continual flouting of school rules	Anything from one to fifteen days	Usually back on trial	Hitting a teacher

What is the function of rules?

Interesting differences were discovered here between high and low excluding schools. Three of the head teachers used the word 'control' to describe the functions of rules in their schools. Of these three head teachers, two were equal first as the highest excluding schools, not only in our study, but in the whole LEA. The school of the third head teacher who referred to 'control' was ranked the fourth highest excluding school in the study. The head teacher of the third highest excluding school used the phrase 'to avoid chaos and to keep order' when describing the function of rules. Thus, all four heads of the four highest excluding schools included either the word 'control' or 'order' in their explanations of the function of school rules, implying that pupils are in need of containment and control. As stated previously, Rutter *et al.* (1979) suggested that schools that exert a high degree of institutional control over children are more effective, but this view was strongly contested by Reynolds and Sullivan (1979), and Galloway (1985) reported that whole staff ownership of and commitment to whichever style (control focused or therapeutic focused) is employed is more important than the type of focus itself. It therefore seems relevant to analyse the individual school ethos responses for all teachers for each school included in the study.

In the case of three head teachers, reference was made to 'learning' and/or 'working' in relation to the function of school rules. Given that the prime task of schools is to ensure that pupils learn to the best of their ability, and to provide pupils with work that will facilitate this, it seems appropriate to consider that a function of rules is to provide a suitable setting and context within which learning and work can take place. Of these three head teachers, two were from the two lowest excluding schools, and the third from one of the schools rated next to lowest. Only one head teacher, who led one of the two lowest excluding schools, used the word 'positive' to describe the function of rules.

How and by whom are rules agreed?

Again, there were clear differences here between high and low excluding schools. Eight head teachers reported that the staff (in one case the 'senior staff') decided upon the school rules. Of these eight, three included the school governors. Four head teachers reported that parents were included in decisions about what the school rules should be and two of these reported that the school council took part in the decision-making process. These four head teachers were from the four lowest excluding schools. This again supports the view of Galloway (1985) that joint and shared ownership of agreed policies and procedures results in those policies and procedures being more effective. Indeed, the head teachers of the three lowest excluding schools all reported that parents, staff and pupils were involved in the decision-making process regarding what the school rules should be. The head teachers of the two highest excluding schools reported that school rules were decided by the staff in one case, and by senior staff and governors in the other case.

Have rules changed?

All the head teachers reported that school rules need to be changed and new rules introduced from time to time in response to social change. In five cases school rules relating to drugs and alcohol had been introduced over the past three years. In two cases (two of the three highest excluding schools) rules relating to knives had been introduced. The head teachers reported that explicit rules regarding drugs, alcohol and knives had only become necessary over the past four or five years. Although there had been implicit understandings prior to this, only when pupils had started to bring knives and drugs into school had a more open and clearer policy been required. One head teacher, from one of the two highest excluding schools, reported that new rules were introduced 'all the time'.

How are rules communicated?

Five head teachers reported that the school rules were to be found in the school handbook. These five included both head teachers from the two highest excluding schools and two from the three lowest excluding schools. Two head teachers reported that the school rules were on display around the school and in classrooms, and one school (one of the two lowest excluding schools) reported that new rules or changes to rules were reported in the minutes of the school council meetings, which were distributed to all pupils, all adults who work at the school and all parents. Five head teachers from the five lowest excluding schools reported that pupils were regularly reminded of the school rules. This relates back to findings by Coulby and Harper

(1985), that in order to contain pupils with challenging behaviours, it is important that school rules should be clear, and understood by all: the first step towards understanding is knowing, and the schools in our study which excluded the fewest pupils were more likely to make sure that the school rules were known to all.

Are rules consistent?

All of the head teachers reported that consistency in administering school rules was desirable. Eight head teachers reported that achieving consistency was very difficult, with two reporting that it was 'impossible' or 'not possible'. One of the head teachers reported that ensuring consistency was particularly difficult among 'weak teachers or newly qualified teachers' (NQTs). The two head teachers who did not report difficulties in ensuring consistency were from the two highest excluding schools. In each of these cases there was the expressed expectation that consistency is possible provided all staff enforce the rules properly.

Is there a place for idiosyncratic rules?

All the head teachers reported that idiosyncratic rules existed in their schools. Two head teachers said that where such rules existed they were usually subject related. By this they were referring to rules that applied specifically, for example, to the use of science or sports equipment, or to behaviour in the art and design technology rooms. Five of the head teachers reported that idiosyncratic rules were 'inevitable' and there were conflicting views as to whether or not it was acceptable to have such rules. One head teacher from one of the two highest excluding schools reported that introduction of idiosyncratic rules was 'not acceptable but happens a lot', suggesting that the head teacher feels powerless to make a difference in this respect, despite his previous optimistic comments about the possibility of achieving consistency in rule enforcement. A head teacher from one of the two lowest excluding schools reported that idiosyncratic rules are 'acceptable to a point'. The head teachers from the other two lowest excluding schools reported that where idiosyncratic rules did exist children had to learn to manage difference and that more important with regard to consistency was consistency *for* all pupils, rather than *from* all teachers. This lack of consistency might be the basis of pupils' low ratings of their school's equality and justice, which was common to both excluded and comparison groups.

What are the basic ground rules?

Basic ground rules were defined as those that were to be adhered to without question, by all pupils and all staff. For nine of the ten head teachers, basic ground rules included those concerned with the safety of the community and the prevention of violence. The remaining head teacher reported 'respect for others' as being the basic ground rule. The phrase 'safety for others' was used by four head teachers. The head teachers from the two highest excluding schools did not refer directly to safety, but were more specific in behavioural terms, reporting 'no drugs, no smoking, no fighting' and 'no drugs, knives and no violence'. These two head teachers, along with the head teacher of the fourth highest excluding school, described ground rules in negative terms (that is using 'no' to pre-fix the rule). The other head teachers presented rules in positive terms – describing behaviours to be encouraged rather than behaviours to be discouraged. This seems to illustrate one difference between schools with a coercive and schools with an incorporative ethos.

Which rules are most difficult to enforce?

All ten head teachers reported that the most difficult rules to enforce in school were those concerned with uniform. This is interesting, as in five cases rules relating to fashion or uniform were reported as being the most common rules. All head teachers described how most pupils deviate from the school uniform in one way or another. Head teachers from four schools felt that this was a normal and healthy response from teenagers who are attempting to assert their own image and identity. Five head teachers reported that they would abandon a strict uniform code if it were not for the fact that parents liked their children to wear school uniform. Five of the head teachers reported 'no smoking' as one of the most difficult rules to enforce and one head teacher (from one of the highest excluding schools) reported 'no fighting' as one of the most difficult rules to enforce. This head teacher reported 'fighting' as one of the criteria for permanent exclusion in his school.

*How does the school respond to parental pressure
to exclude?*

Head teachers from the four highest excluding schools all reported that the views of other parents did influence or 'sway' the head's decision to exclude disruptive pupils. This is perhaps indicative of a weak boundary between subsystems. The other head teachers reported that parents' views were important but did not influence the final decision to exclude. The head teachers of the three lowest excluding schools were clear that it is the head teacher's decision whether or not to exclude, indicative, we feel, of a mature ability to draw boundaries, to know where the responsibility lies, and to accept that responsibility. One of these head teachers made the point that other parents usually do not know the full facts and that, due to matters of confidentiality, it is not always possible to share the details with them.

Are there set criteria for fixed term exclusions?

Five of the head teachers reported that fixed term exclusions were most commonly given when a pupil persistently broke the school rules. Four head teachers used the word 'persistent' and three (two from the two highest excluding schools) the word 'offences'. These two head teachers also gave explicit, behavioural examples of when fixed term exclusions would be given: for 'smoking, fighting, not turning up for detention and truanting', and for 'failing to attend detention, for fighting and for receiving two demerits for uniform deviance'. The head teachers of the two lowest excluding schools reported that fixed term exclusions were given 'when other sanctions have made no difference', and 'through discussion with parents, and for a cooling off period'. These differences again reflect the difference between a coercive and an incorporative ethos.

Is there a set criterion for their length?

The head teachers of the two lowest excluding schools reported that fixed term exclusions were normally for no more than two or three days. They both presented the view that it was never good for pupils to miss school, and that for most incidents which resulted in a fixed term exclusion, a two- or three-day exclusion was sufficient to acknowledge the seriousness of the situation, and to keep the pupil engaged in school and not to miss too much work. One of them reported that excluded pupils miss a great deal of class work and, upon their return, are at a greater disadvantage than before they were excluded. The other eight head teachers reported that the length of time of the fixed term exclusion depended upon the circumstances and/or the nature or severity of the reason for the exclusion. The head teacher of one of the highest excluding schools said that the length of exclusion 'depends upon the severity of the crime' and that it could be for five days or for fifteen days. The head teacher of the third highest excluding school reported that the fixed term exclusion could be 'anything from one to fifteen days'.

Are there agreed arrangements for pupils returning to school?

Seven head teachers reported that a meeting would be set up prior to the pupil's return to school, with the parent(s) and either the head teacher or the head of year. In the case of five schools this meeting would include the pupil. One head teacher said that the parents would be written to but that the pupil would be expected to return to school on the agreed day and to go straight back into class. This was also the case with one of the lowest excluding schools, except that the parent(s) would first meet with the head teacher. The head teacher of one of the highest excluding schools referred to a joint meeting with parents, head teacher and pupil as a 'final warning meeting', and the head teacher of the third highest excluding school reported that the pupil would 'usually be allowed back on trial'. The head teacher of the other of the two lowest excluding schools described how the head of year and school counsellor would set up a re-integration programme for the pupil. This was the only head teacher who referred to setting up a special plan for the returning pupil.

Is there a set criterion for permanent exclusions?

All head teachers reported that acts of violence to an adult or pupil would lead to a permanent exclusion. Some head teachers, including all three from the lowest excluding schools, made a distinction between a very serious or serious or severe attack and a lesser act of violence and whether or not the violent act was towards a teacher or a pupil. The head teacher of one of the highest excluding schools reported that a permanent exclusion would automatically follow the bringing into school of drugs or a knife. This head teacher was clear that this was an unconditional rule and there would be no exceptions. The head teacher of the other highest excluding school reported that a permanent exclusion would also be given if a pupil persistently failed to produce satisfactory work, or was a persistent truant. One head teacher reported that the 'constant disruption of other pupils' would result in a permanent exclusion.

None of the head teachers reported that an accumulation of fixed term exclusions would lead to a permanent exclusion. However, it may be implicit that the continued use of the word 'persistent' and 'constant' would suggest that permanently excluded pupils would already have received at least one fixed term exclusion. The head teacher of the third lowest excluding school reported that permanent exclusion would follow 'a very serious incident which would be unlikely to be an isolated incident'. Of the twenty pupils in the study who had been permanently excluded, five had previously received three fixed term exclusions, and three had received two; one of these three had also been permanently excluded from another school. The remaining twelve pupils had never previously received either a fixed term or permanent exclusion.

Summary of questionnaire and interview data

Analysis of the pupil questionnaires from the excluded and comparison groups showed that there was no difference between the groups for the four characteristics of pupil morale, physical environment, equality and justice and extra-curricular activities. We were particularly interested in the fact that there was no difference between the pupil groups in respect of equality and justice, given that all pupils in the excluded group felt that their exclusion from school had been unfair and that they had not been to blame. One explanation for this may be found in the low scores which both groups gave for equality and justice, suggesting that neither group considered equality and justice in school to be fair and just. The two groups differed in respect of teacher job satisfaction, the learning context, teacher–pupil relations and discipline, with the excluded group presenting less favourable views. In their more negative responses with respect to the learning context of the school, the excluded group would seem to be responding to their own direct experience rather than the more general aspect of the learning context for all pupils in the school. The fact that the excluded pupils and the comparison pupils differed in respect of teacher job satisfaction, teacher–pupil relations and discipline is less surprising given that the excluded pupils are more likely to have experienced first hand teacher frustration in respect of their behaviour in school, and that this is likely to be seen by the pupils as teachers feeling less satisfied with their jobs as teachers, and resulting in poorer relationships between teachers and them as pupils. It also would appear that, although the questions relating to these themes were presented in general rather than specific statements (e.g. 'teachers treat pupils fairly' rather than 'teachers treat me fairly'), pupils in both groups may have responded from their own personal experiences of how teachers treat them.

The parents of the excluded group and the comparison group differed significantly on all school ethos characteristics with the exception of the physical environment. The parents of the excluded pupils felt more negatively than the parents of the comparison pupils for pupil morale, teacher job satisfaction, the learning context, teacher–pupil relations, equality and justice, school leadership, discipline, information to parents and parent–teacher consultation. The excluded parents' responses to the school ethos questionnaires tend to reflect the views of their children that external factors (in this case, the school) were at fault with respect to their children's difficulties.

One explanation for the overwhelming difference between the two groups of parents, with the parents of the excluded group presenting more negatively for all indicators, may lie directly in the exclusion of their child from the school. Had these parents completed the questionnaire before their child had been excluded a more favourable response may have been presented. However, this post-exclusion picture of how these parents now view the school is important and valid. In our interviews with these parents, two parents referred to help and support which they had received from the school, and in some cases, although parents were upset and anxious, and in some cases angry about their child's exclusion, they did not express their views as comprehensively negative as they did in the school ethos questionnaires. One explanation for this may be that, when talking face to face with us about their child, parents may have felt more encouraged to focus upon the specific details and more intimate aspects of the exclusion and their family experiences, whereas, when completing the questionnaires relating specifically to the school from where their child was excluded, their more angry feelings were aroused, reinforcing their view that more could have been done for their child, and that the school had 'failed' their child. This may highlight the fact that a different emphasis of a response can emerge depending upon the methods of data collection. It is not that the parents' responses to the questionnaires contradicted their responses to the different, but related, questions asked in the face-to-face interview, but rather that the presentation of a questionnaire provides a context where the parents could provide a more extreme view of their anger and disappointment.

The responses of the teachers who completed the school ethos questionnaires differed mainly in respect of teacher status, although the data is fundamentally flawed given the fact that the two highest excluding schools did not return the teacher questionnaires. Across all schools the lowest status teachers (newly qualified and main scale) were more negative in respect of nine of the twelve indicators of school ethos. Three of these, the learning context, teacher–pupil relations and discipline, support the responses given by the excluded pupils. In addition, they reported negatively on equality and justice, which supports the low ethos reports of both the excluded and the comparison pupils. The three characteristics which the lowest status teachers reported as positive school ethos were extra-curricular activities, teacher job satisfaction and teacher morale – their ratings of these three characteristics are in direct contrast to the responses of the highest status teachers (head teachers and deputy head teachers) who reported these as being the least positive school ethos characteristics of their school. The highest status teachers supported the views of the excluded pupils with respect to teacher job satisfaction.

The head teachers' responses to the semi-structured interview show that there was evidence of differences between the highest and lowest excluding schools in respect of language used to describe their school, supporting the work of Reynolds and Sullivan (1981) described earlier. The head teachers of the highest excluding schools used words such as 'control' and 'enforce' compared with the head teachers of the lowest excluding schools who used words such as 'provide a positive learning setting' and 'civilised living as a learning community' when describing the function of rules in their school. There were some common aspects across all schools in respect of the head teachers' responses. For example, all head teachers acknowledged that it is very difficult to ensure consistency between the staff when putting the school rules into practice, although the highest two excluding schools felt that it should not be difficult if staff did their job properly. There was also agreement on the basic ground rules for all schools, although again the language used by head teachers varied, with the head teachers of the two lowest excluding schools using more general, less specific language, e.g. 'respect for others' safety', and head teachers of the highest excluding schools offering more specific language, e.g. 'no drugs, no fighting, no crimes'. However, the overall consensus across all schools with respect to basic ground rules was concerned with safety. There was consensus across all schools in respect of new rules introduced, with all head teachers offering specifics such as 'uniform' and 'fashion' and 'drugs' and 'alcohol'. In every case 'smoking' and/or 'uniform' were presented as being the most difficult school rules to enforce, with one head teacher of one of the two highest excluding schools reporting the 'no fighting' rule as being difficult to enforce. There were differences between the highest and lowest excluding schools also with respect to how school rules are made. Only in the cases of the three lowest excluding schools were pupils reported to be involved in the decision about school rules.

The data presented in this chapter has demonstrated not only differences between schools in respect of the rules, or codes of behaviour, by which the pupils are expected to conform, but also, perhaps more significantly, differences within schools. Children who have little experience of boundary setting, who have external locus of control and who struggle generally to experience the learning part of school life in a positive way, will be especially vulnerable to these inconsistencies. In such circumstances these vulnerable pupils are likely to feel anxious and uncontained.

Chapter 6

Four case studies of excluded pupils

Social behaviour is not reducible to general laws but rather to situational analyses which take account of the system members' attribution of meaning in different contexts. For example, in our study, it would have been possible, as with many previous studies, to have addressed one or two aspects of an excluded pupil's life (one or two subsystems) and tried to make some sense of the findings in isolation from the other subsystems. The question then would be what real sense or practical usefulness could be made from findings which only account for a part of the story? Hearing one side of the story can produce convincing and seductive 'evidence' but obtaining data from each of the interrelating systems more usefully presents the story as it really is – complex, confusing and contradictory, but nonetheless a more realistic picture than any single separate account.

What follows in this chapter are individual case studies of four of the twenty excluded children from our study. These case studies include, for each child, details all of the factors which we considered for the within-child, within-family and within-school variables of the study, and aim to demonstrate an integrated and holistic picture of each child. Included in the case studies are the different accounts about the exclusion given by the children themselves, their parents and their head teachers. In our study we found that these different stories provided some of the richest information about different perspectives and beliefs, and about the different positions held within and across the systems. Throughout this book we have already included extracts from these stories in order to emphasis specific points, but we include them here in more depth to illustrate how the different accounts complemented or contradicted each other. It is important to note that we were not concerned with eliciting 'truth', but rather to regard the differing perspectives of the same incident or set of incidents as being indicative of the existence of multiple truths. Pupils, parents and head teachers may indeed share a common goal – to make the best of the educational opportunities available to pupils. However, their different roles, positions and perspectives on how this can be achieved will inevitably sometimes differ. Thus an interpretation of a particular event is likely to hold a different meaning, a different 'truth', for the different parties involved.

The following case studies have been selected at random (every fifth referral) from the twenty excluded pupils in the study, and include three boys and one girl. A full description of each child's within-child data is included, as are details of each child's family circumstances, including the presence or absence of family risk factors and family resilience. Information regarding the school ethos is included as well as the stories of the exclusion as mentioned above. These four case studies, although taken at random from the total sample, may seem to the reader to be the most extreme cases. Table 6.1 shows individual profiles of all 40 children in the study, excluded and comparison. The excluded group can be seen overwhelmingly to experience a greater number of challenges and difficulties than the children in the comparison group.

Kevin

Kevin is a mixed race Muslim 13-year-old boy living with his mother and younger sister at the time of his exclusion from school. He is seventh in a family of eight children. He had been excluded from his school in Year 7 and had been out of school for six weeks when we first met him and his mother.

Kevin's scores on the cognitive abilities test placed him within the low average range of general ability, and showed a particular difficulty in his verbal comprehension and reading and spelling skills. His mother told us that she had been concerned about Kevin's reading when he had been in his primary school, and she recalled that he had received some help then. Since starting at his secondary school he had continued to find reading difficult, and his mother said that the books which he had to read were much too hard for him. She had told him to ask the teacher for some extra help but didn't think that he had received any. When we talked to Kevin about his reading he told us that there were things at school which he did have difficulty reading, especially in some lessons, but that he felt that he couldn't really ask his teachers for help with reading. He demonstrated low global self-esteem score, with particularly low scores in the domains of scholastic, behaviour, romantic and athletic self-esteem. This picture of how Kevin sees himself was supported by his head teacher and by his mother, and suggests that Kevin did wish to be more successful in these particular areas than he felt himself to be.

In respect of locus of control Kevin demonstrated considerable externality, being unable to express any thoughts about what he might have been able to do differently which might have prevented his exclusion from school. He had a tendency to blame others for all the difficulties which he had encountered, including his teachers for not helping him enough with his reading, and his mother's limited English language skills for her not being able to help him when he got into trouble and when the school decided to exclude him.

When we talked to Kevin's mother about the family we learnt that she had married at 17, and that it had been a difficult marriage. She and Kevin's father had separated five years earlier, and divorced about eighteen months ago. She explained that she is Turkish and came over to the UK to work after she left school and lived with relatives. Her mother and stepfather had come to London a few years later and now live nearby. She told us that she had met her husband quite soon after arriving in London to live. She remembered herself as being innocent and immature at that time, and became pregnant quite early in their relationship. She described the marriage as being difficult, and that on several occasions she had returned to live with her mother and stepfather, taking her children with her. Each time she went back to her husband she had become pregnant. They eventually had eight children, and she described how this had put a great strain on her marriage and on their housing situation. They were living in a three-bedroomed apartment which she described as 'damp and horrible'. She told us that her husband had at times been physically aggressive towards her but never towards the children, and seldom in front of them. She remembered Kevin saying things to her about not letting dad hurt her, but she doesn't think that he knew much at the time about what was happening, and probably doesn't remember much now.

When Kevin was 13 months he and two older siblings went to stay with their maternal grandmother and step-grandfather, who lived in a nearby borough. This was due to the family's poor housing and accommodation difficulties. Kevin's parents were trying to get rehoused in the local authority where the grandparents were living.

Table 6.1 Profiles of within-child, within-family and within-school factors in excluded and comparison pupils

	Excluded pupils									
	Within-child factors						Within-family factors		Within-school factors	
Name	Cognitive ability <85	Verbal ability difficulties	Literacy scores <8yrs. 5mths.	No.of-ve self-esteem domains	Locus of control	Support	No. of family risk factors	Family resilience high/low	No.of-ve school ethos ratings by pupils	School rank for exclusions 1 = highest
Stephen	Yes	Yes	No	3	External	Peers	2	Low	3	5=
Simon	No	No	No	3	Internal	Peers, parents	4	Low	3	9=
Peter	No	No	Yes	3	Internal	Peers	2	Low	3	5=
Philip	Yes	No	Yes	5	External	None	3	Low	3	4
Kevin	Yes	Yes	Yes	4	External	Peers	6	Low	4	1=
David	No	No	No	5	External	None	2	Low	3	5=
Craig	Yes	Yes	Yes	3	External	None	5	Low	3	8
Darren	Yes	Yes	No	4	External	Peers, parents	3	Low	4	5=
John	No	No	No	3	Internal	Parents	2	Low	4	3
Terry	No	Yes	Yes	4	External	Peers	8	Low	4	1=

Jack	No	No	No	2	Internal	None	3	Low	3	5=
Kharm	Yes	Yes	No	3	Internal	None	0	Low	2	4
Gary	No	No	No	3	External	Peers	3	Low	3	9=
Matt	No	No	No	5	External	Peers	3	Low	3	5=
Jade	No	No	Yes	4	External	None	4	Low	4	1=
Adam	No	No	No	4	External	None	1	Low	4	1=
Julie	Yes	Yes	No	4	External	Parents	1	Low	4	4
Nicola	Yes	Yes	Yes	4	External	Peers, parents	7	Low	3	8
Sarah	No	No	No	3	External	Peers, parents, teacher	3	Low	3	5=
Warren	No	No	Yes	4	External	Parents, peers	4	Low	3	6=

Continued

Tasble 6.1 continued

| | Within-child factors | | | | Comparison pupils | | Within-family factors | | Within-school factors | |
| | | | | | | | | | | |
Name	Cognitive ability < 85	Verbal ability difficulties	Literacy scores < 8yrs. 5mths.	No. of -ve self-esteem domains	Locus of control	Support	No. of family risk factors	Family resilience high/low	No. of -ve school ethos ratings by pupils	School rank for exclusions 1 = highest
Tom	No	No	No	2	Internal	Teachers, parents, peers	1	High	3	5=
Clive	No	No	No	2	Internal	Teachers, parents, peers	2	High	3	9=
Michael	No	No	No	1	External	Peers	2	High	3	5=
Robert	Yes	Yes	No	1	Internal	Parents, teachers, peers	1	High	2	4
Graham	No	No	Yes	3	Internal	Parents, peers	1	High	2	1=
Jamie	No	No	No	2	Internal	Parents, peers	4	High	1	5=
Steve	No	No	Yes	4	External	Peers	2	High	4	8=
Alan	No	No	No	2	External	Parents, teachers	0	High	3	5=

Will	No	No	No	2	External	Parents, teachers, peers	2	High	3	3
Trevor	No	No	No	1	Internal	Parents, teachers, peers	1	Low	3	1=
Stuart	No	No	No	2	Internal	Parents, peers	2	High	3	5=
Gerhal	No	Yes	No	2	Internal	Parents, peers	2	Low	2	4
Guy	No	No	No	1	External	Parents, peers	4	High	3	9=
Brad	No	No	Yes	2	Internal	Parents, teachers, peers	2	High	3	5=
Jane	No	No	No	1	Internal	Parents, teachers, peers	2	High	3	1=
Brian	No	No	No	2	Internal	Parents, teachers, peers	0	High	4	1=
Clare	No	No	Yes	1	Internal	Parents, teachers, peers	0	High	3	4
Sharon	No	No	No	1	Internal	Peers	1	High	3	8
Paula	No	No	No	1	Internal	Parents, peers	1	High	3	5=
Chris	No	No	No	2	Internal	Parents, teachers, peers	3	High	3	6=

Kevin's mother told us that the three children stayed with her parents for much longer than she had intended, but she became pregnant again and was unable to have them back home. Kevin was three years old when the family eventually secured their rehousing in the local authority of their choice. Kevin's mother explained to us that Kevin had wanted to stay with his grandparents although the two other children were happy to return home. Kevin had cried for his grandmother and started to wet the bed. She told us that she had understood his distress and had thought seriously about letting him stay with his grandparents. However, the grandmother's husband had said that he did not want the children to stay, although she felt that her mother would have agreed.

We were told that Kevin and his younger sister still see their father, although not at regular times, and Kevin never talks to his mother about him. Their father shows an interest in the children's education and has attended meetings at school to try to help with the difficulties which Kevin had at school.

We asked about Kevin's earliest experiences, as an infant, and learnt that he had been a premature birth, born six weeks early. He had been kept in special care and mother had left hospital without him. He had developed asthma and eczema at about two years of age, and had also experienced a couple of fits. He was referred to the local paediatrician and had been seen regularly, but he had grown out of both the fitting and of the eczema although he still suffered from asthma. He had been taken into hospital on a couple of occasions for severe asthmatic attacks, once from school and once in the middle of the night from home. His mother told us that Kevin had been a very clingy child and it had always been difficult for her to leave him at nursery. He would scream and shout for her to stay with him or to take him home. The teacher had told her that she needed to be firm with him and walk away quickly without looking back, but she said that she had found this impossible to do. She had wanted to go into the room with him to get him settled, and then leave him, but the teacher had said that it would be much better if she left him at the door. The teacher had told Kevin's mother that she couldn't allow all the mothers to come into the room, and that the other children would be upset if she came in with Kevin when their mothers were not allowed in. Kevin's mother told us that she believes that this was really the start of Kevin being unhappy at school. He had never really settled and she blames herself for not challenging the teacher, or for not finding Kevin a different nursery. She had not told the nursery that Kevin had lived with his grandmother during his early years as she did not think that it was relevant to his reluctance to leave her to go to nursery. Throughout his education Kevin's mother told us that she had never been advised to seek outside help for Kevin, and the school had not referred him to their educational psychologist or to the local child guidance service.

We talked about things which were happening in the family around the time of Kevin's exclusion from school. Kevin's mother couldn't think of anything which she considered to be especially important or different at that time, except the worries around Kevin's behaviour at school and the exclusion itself. After some reflection she remembered that it had been a particularly difficult time because she had also been worried about her stepfather who had recently had a heart attack. She was having to visit him in hospital as well as look after her mother. We asked if Kevin had perhaps also been worried about his grandfather. She thought that he must have been because they had been very close, although he hadn't talked to her about being worried. She had tried to talk to him about not getting into so much trouble at school because it was adding to the upset in the family, but he hadn't seemed to be able to improve. The day that he was eventually excluded Kevin had called her on her mobile phone to tell her. She was on her way to the hospital to take her mother and had been torn between taking her mother and going home to see Kevin. She decided to continue with the visit to the hospital and not to tell her mother, who was already worried about her husband's health. Kevin's step-grandfather died three weeks after Kevin's exclusion from school.

In terms of family risk factors, Kevin's family had experienced six of the eight factors that were focused upon in the study. He had been separated from his mother whilst in the special care unit immediately after his premature birth, and had only been allowed home six weeks later. He had been separated again from her when he had lived with his grandmother for nearly two years (although he did see her often) and then experienced separation from his grandmother when he was three years of age (although again, he continued to see her often). Although his mother had stayed in hospital for two weeks after his birth and had visited him daily, she had not been able to hold him or nurse him for the first week, and had not been able to breastfeed him at all. It is important to acknowledge that Kevin effectively experienced three periods of maternal separation – he was separated twice from his natural mother, at birth when he was in special care, and again at the age of 13 months when he went to live with his grandparents, and then from his grandmother, who had been his main carer until the age of 3 years.

Other family risk factors were his parents' divorce, the regular absence of his father during his early childhood, his own serious asthmatic condition which had required emergency hospital admission on a couple of occasions, and his maternal step-grandfather's serious illness which had been of concern to his mother and grandmother, and very possibly to Kevin himself, during the lead-up to his exclusion, and his death a short time later.

An analysis of the interviews with Kevin and his mother showed the family to have a low resilience to family risk factors. Of the seven characteristics of resilience Kevin's family demonstrated overall difficulties in a comprehensive understanding of events, in being able to tell a coherent account of events which they described, and in the family's ability to be flexible in the face of difficulty. In addition, Kevin's mother reported that she had not had a positive school experience herself, and remembers being very unhappy at school and wanting to leave as soon as possible (which she did). She reported Kevin as being a sickly and difficult baby, which, she said, is also how her own mother had felt about him when he had been living with her.

Kevin and his mother shared similar views about the ethos of the school from which he had been excluded. They both felt that there was poor equality and justice in the school, particularly in relation to the Turkish boys. Perhaps surprisingly Kevin was more positive than his mother about the discipline in the school. They both felt negatively about the learning environment, feeling that Kevin in particular had not received the help he had needed, but feeling also that other children with similar difficulties had also needed more help than they were given.

The pupils, parents and head teachers were each asked to recall the exclusion, and to give their own accounts of the reason for it including their recollections of the events which led up to it and followed. What follows are the accounts of Kevin, his mother and his head teacher, and a discussion of the similarities and differences.

Kevin's story

Kevin explained that someone was playing the game of 'dare' and some boys in a year above him hit one of his friends on the head, and then 'it all got a bit nasty' and his friend got hurt and they all 'got into a fight and it got ugly'. He said that he was sent to the deputy head teacher's office and had to sit with the deputy head teacher for a couple of hours. The head teacher gave him a note which said that he was excluded from school. Kevin said that he had been in some trouble in the lower part of the school for 'mucking about with the tennis nets', but since he went into the upper part he had 'got better' and hadn't been in any trouble. Kevin said that he did not have any warning about the exclusion. He said that when he was given a letter by the school to give to his mother saying that he had been excluded, he thought he had better telephone her to warn her. He said that his mother does not read English very well so he had to explain to her what the letter said. Kevin said that he does not think that he should have been permanently excluded. He said that he felt very upset at the time of the exclusion. Kevin could not think of any good things about being excluded from school and described the disadvantages as being bored at home, of not getting a good education and worrying about not getting a good job.

Kevin told us that he really wanted to go to another school but that he didn't know how to go about making this happen, and said that he would like some help. He explained to me that his mother speaks 'reasonably OK English' but that she did not go to school in England and therefore 'doesn't understand the system'. He said that he felt that his parents wanted to help him but that they were not in a position to. He felt strongly that schools should not exclude pupils permanently, but that if there was a problem they should send them home for a short time 'but not for good'.

Kevin said that he was only out of school for one week before he started to attend the unit, which he attended three times a week and which he was enjoying, but he was also missing school and couldn't understand why he couldn't go to another school.

Kevin's mother's story

Kevin's mother told us that she first heard about Kevin's exclusion when he had telephoned her on her mobile phone. Kevin had then brought home a letter from the school. She said that Kevin had to read her the letter as she has difficulty reading English. She said that his problems first started when he began secondary school and that she only knew about this when she had attended a parents' evening. She felt that Kevin had been picked on by teachers and that every time there had been a problem the school would blame Kevin, even when he wasn't there. She had been told by the school to find another school for him as the teachers said that he was not happy at the school and that a different school might be better for him. She told us that she had tried to find another school but they could not find one, and the school had not suggested or recommended where she should try. She said that Kevin had had some learning difficulties and 'his friends make him do things'. She described Kevin as being 'very easily led'.

Kevin's mother said that she had gone to the school herself with a friend as soon as she had received the letter about the exclusion, and had asked the school not to exclude him. She wanted the school to help her to find another school for Kevin and not to exclude him, as she knew that if he had a bad record she would never be able to find another school to take him. She said that she was very angry with the school and said that Kevin is a very good boy and that he had never been a problem at home.

Kevin's mother told us the whole family was very upset but Kevin was the most upset. He liked school and he really missed going. He had always liked school even though he found the work difficult. He now attended to a unit where he is no trouble. She told us that nobody helped her when Kevin was excluded and 'because I don't speak good English I did not know what to do or where to go'.

Kevin's head teacher's story

Kevin's head teacher explained to us that he tended to leave the details of exclusions from the school to his deputies, and that he would 'come in at the last moment, really to referee and support my staff'. He told us that he could not recall Kevin's exclusion specifically but that there had been a group of boys, mainly Turkish, who had started to 'run amok and things got out of hand a bit'. He thought that Kevin was one of these, and two or three of them had been excluded at the same time. He described it as 'a bit of a cull'.

He told us that he did not exclude pupils readily and, although they had had a 'spate' over the past year, this was unusual. He was confident that his heads of year and deputy heads made sensible and fair judgements and he had never had cause to question their decisions when they recommended a permanent exclusion. He said that the school governors felt the same about his judgement and that they had always supported him.

We asked if he there had been an opportunity for him to meet with

Kevin's mother. He said that he had not done this, but that he would have done so if she had made a request to meet him. He was sure that she had met with his deputy.

Discussion

These three accounts of Kevin's exclusion highlight how the different perspectives and positions relate differently to the situation. In this case the head teacher presents a detached account of distancing himself from the Kevin's exclusion, trusting his deputies to make recommendations which he felt he had no need to question. He had not attempted to meet with Kevin's parents, although he did say that he would have done so had they requested a meeting. There is an acknowledgement that Kevin was probably one of the Turkish boys whom he had excluded. There was no acknowledgement of possible difficulties which Turkish parents may experience in an English school system and procedures.

The head teacher made no mention of Kevin's learning difficulties and there was an overall sense from the interview that he saw himself as confirming the recommendations of his senior staff, and that he had the full support of the school's governing body.

Kevin's and his mother's accounts suggest a situation of helplessness, with them both feeling strongly that Kevin should not have been excluded, but Kevin feeling that his parents had been unable to help him, and his mother saying that she did not know what to do or where to go for help for Kevin.

In this description of Kevin, his family circumstances, his mother's views and accounts her own experience of Kevin's education and exclusion, and his head teacher's story, there is little overt acknowledgement of interrelating systems. They each present their own version and memories of events, including who or what might have been to blame, and what could and should have been done differently. Kevin's mother had told us that he had not experienced difficulties until he had started secondary school, yet she had also shared with us his early difficulties of separating from her to go to nursery school. It seems that she had been unable to connect the two situations. The connecting of school and home events can only be made if there is awareness in each system of the different events. In Kevin's case the nursery staff had been unaware of Kevin's earliest experiences of separation from his mother. Parents understandably do not always inform their child's school of difficulties in the family. They may feel that these are private matters, or they may underestimate the impact of home events upon a child's school life.

Terry

Terry is a 14-year-old black African-Caribbean boy living with his older brother, mother and stepfather at the time of the exclusion. He had been excluded from his secondary school when he was in Year 9.

In the cognitive assessment Terry had demonstrated good average ability in most of the subtests in the assessment, with the exception of expressive and receptive language skills, where he performed well below average. He had age-appropriate reading skills although he demonstrated some difficulty with spelling. In respect of his self-esteem, Terry demonstrated a strong positive self-esteem in the athletic, social acceptance and romantic domains, but was more negative in the domains of scholastic and behaviour self-esteem and global self-worth. He had felt positively about the support which he received from his class mates but less positively about the support which the school gave him, and about the support which his mother and stepfather had been able to give him with school.

He also demonstrated a highly external locus of control, blaming other pupils and the school for the difficulties which he found himself in. He was unable to share with us any thoughts about how he might have behaved and acted differently which might have prevented his exclusion. Terry was very upset by his exclusion, which he told us had come as a great shock to him, and which he felt to be unfair.

In conversation with Terry's mother we discovered that the family had experienced all eight of the family risk factors which we were considering. Her marriage to Terry's father had broken down shortly after Terry was born and she had lived on her own with her two children until she married her current husband seven years ago. Terry had experienced a two-month separation from his mother at the age of 18 months when she was seriously injured in a car accident. Terry and his brother were looked after by their mother's sister as, at the time, Terry's mother was a single parent. She was in a specialist spinal injury hospital some distance from her home and saw the boys only at weekends when her parents brought them to visit her. She told us that she remembered this being an upsetting time as the boys had wanted to climb onto her bed and cuddle her but she had been in too much physical pain for them to do this.

She described how the boys were very upset at first but later when they visited her they would virtually ignore her, playing with other children on the ward.

We asked Terry's mother about his earliest experiences. He had been born a week early but had been healthy and strong. She had taken him home from hospital after two days, but she had suffered from post-natal depression and experienced difficulty managing Terry and his three-year-old brother. She had separated from Terry's father during the late stages of her pregnancy but had received a lot of help from her parents and from her two sisters who lived nearby. She told us that she doesn't remember very much about Terry as a baby, other than that he did not cry very much and was 'a good baby'. She told us that he had become a more difficult child after she had been in hospital. She told us that she thinks that her sister had a different routine than her and treated her own children differently, so that when she looked after Terry and his brother when she was in hospital the boys had found it difficult to adjust back to living with her. Terry had attended a playgroup and the nursery class in his local school, and she remembered that he had not enjoyed going and would cling to her at the school gate. She told us that she could not stay at home with him as she needed to work. Her mother would collect the boys from school and she would collect them from her mother's flat when she finished work.

Terry had suffered from severe eczema and his mother reported that he was often quite distressed, especially in the summer months when he would scratch his arms and break the skin.

Terry's family demonstrated low resilience characteristics, particularly in the areas of coherence, a cognitive understanding of events and an ability to present a positive view of negative events. Terry's mother told us that she had enjoyed school when she was in her primary school but had not enjoyed her secondary school at all. She said that she 'couldn't wait to leave'. She later told us that the school from which Terry had been excluded was the same school she had attended as a pupil. She told us that there were a couple of teachers who were still there and who remembered her. She said that she had found this quite difficult, as she had felt more like a pupil than a parent whenever she had to visit the school.

Terry and his mother did not share a common view of the ethos of Terry's school. Terry had a more positive view of the school, whereas his mother rated it negatively on all school ethos indicators. Terry felt positively in respect of teacher job satisfaction, extra-curricular activities, pupil morale and the physical environment. He felt less positively in respect of the school's equality and justice and discipline.

Terry's story

Terry explained that he had had two previous exclusions for talking in school and he thinks that the school just got fed up with him. The final exclusion came as a big surprise to him and his mother. He said that the school didn't give a particular reason. He said that he had been 'on report' for ages and comments were all fine. Terry found out in the middle of the day from the deputy head that he had spoken to his mother on the telephone and that Terry had now been permanently excluded. Terry said that he was very upset and 'couldn't quite believe it'. He said that he ran out of school and did not stay until the end of the day, even though the deputy head had told him to report to his office at the end of the day to collect a letter. Terry said that he still does not know why he was excluded on that day. He remembers going to his mother's work and that she was also very upset. He told me that his mother refused to attend the governors' meeting as she said that they'd already made up their minds.

Terry told me that his grandparents, who live with the family, were very upset, and that his stepfather didn't say anything. Terry's school friends rang him up but friends who attended a different school did not know, and Terry pretended to them that he was still attending school.

When I asked Terry if there had been anyone in school who could have helped him, he explained that there were a couple of teachers with whom he got on well, but that they 'were not senior enough to help'. He described how some teachers did not have enough 'power' to have helped him. Terry said that he had never been involved in a fight at school and had never sworn at a teacher although he felt that teachers would describe his behaviour as 'rude and disruptive'. He feels that he should not have been excluded, and 'certainly not without a warning'. Terry also felt that because he was on report for so long he had to behave all the time and that any little thing he did, which other boys also did, was written on his report. He felt he had to be 100 per cent perfect and that 'is not in my nature'. Terry wants to go to another school as soon as possible. He recognised that he had lost a choice of his GCSE options, even if he gets into another school. Terry felt strongly that schools should not be allowed to exclude pupils in Year 9, as it is such an important year.

Terry told me that he did not think that his being black was anything to do with the way he was treated by the school. He felt that teachers did not like him stating his own opinion, even though he felt he was not rude. He felt that other pupils were much ruder. Terry said that he had tried to tell his mother that he was unhappy at the school but that she had not really listened to him. He feels that he probably had not told her forcefully enough and then 'it was too late'.

Terry's mother's story

Terry's mother felt that Terry never had what she would call 'serious' difficulties and she had been very supportive of the school. The school had called in the educational psychologist but she felt that this was a 'waste of time'. She felt that Terry's behaviour was something which the school could have 'easily dealt with'. She explained that she has never had any problems with Terry at home and that at school 'there were all these adults and yet they were ringing me up about every petty little thing'. Terry's mother described several incidents where she felt the school had overreacted to what she considered to be a minor incident. One example she gave was receiving a letter from school about Terry throwing paper out of the classroom window. She said 'it became so petty'. She had the impression that the school was 'looking for something to get Terry out of the school' – she said 'that's what it boiled down to'. She said that the school said that they had tried very hard but she is not sure that this was true. She felt that she had not received any warning. She described Terry as being so stressed when he was excluded. She said that 'he had lost everything – his personality and everything and he was very down'. She had told Terry to tell the school how he felt but she said he felt they wouldn't understand.

Terry's mother told us that there had been no specific incident which had led to the permanent exclusion, but 'disruptive behaviour' was the reason given. She said that the psychologist he saw was also a tutor at the school and that Terry was told that he had to have counselling from her. She told us 'something had happened with Terry and this lady' and she had telephoned the school to find out what had happened. She said that the head of year had promised to find out and ring her back. She waited for two days and he did not ring, so she had telephoned again. Terry had told his mother that the counsellor had told him that he was wasting everybody's time. She felt that this comment was inappropriate but when she eventually spoke with the head of year he had not mentioned this but instead told her that the school was permanently excluding Terry. Terry's mother told us that she was so annoyed that she did not bother to attend the governors' meeting, but instead she wrote a letter to 'all and sundry' saying that as far as she was concerned she had been very supportive of the school and was outraged that they should permanently exclude Terry for disruptive behaviour. She said that if Terry had been violent or swearing or taking drugs, she could have understood the school's actions. She told us that she received no response to her letters. She believed that the school 'never got to know the real Terry'.

Terry's mother remembered Terry coming to her workplace when he had been sent home from school and how upset and distressed he was. She felt that there had been no one to help her or Terry at the time. She had hoped that the educational psychologist might have been able to help but she had not. Terry's mother was very critical of the educational psychologist and felt that she was there to help the school and not to help Terry. She felt that the school had just wanted to 'get rid of Terry', and that she has had to do all the work with finding another school as soon as possible. Three months later he had been offered a place at a unit, but not a school. She had thought that the education authority would find him another school and 'that would be that', but she said she did not realise that parents have to find another school. She had been told by the education department that Terry would have to go to the unit before he could go to another school. She thought that the education department would be on the side of parents and children but she now feels that they just support the schools. She felt that parents were on their own at times like this, and that there was no one to advise her.

Terry's head teacher's story

Terry's head teacher was very clear that there had been no alternative but to permanently exclude Terry. She said that he had been persistently disruptive in school over the past two years. He had not taken full advantage of his meeting with the school counsellor who had been seeing him weekly for a term prior to his exclusion. She described Terry as being 'a self-opinionated young man' and that 'his mother is rather the same'. She was also clear to point out to us that her decision to exclude Terry had nothing to do with his colour. She explained that they were a multicultural school and that 'all pupils are expected to keep to the rules irrespective of their colour'.

His head teacher said that Terry had spent a long time on school report and that his report was often marred by comments from teachers about his 'silly behaviour'. She felt that the school had given Terry many chances and that 'we had come to the end of our patience'. She had been disappointed that Terry's parents had not shown up at the governors' meeting and that the governors had no choice 'under the circumstances' but to confirm the exclusion. She told us that the governors did not automatically confirm exclusions and that in recent months they had asked her to reconsider her recommendation on two occasions. As a consequence she had readmitted one pupil who was now 'doing well'. Terry's head teacher did not know whether or not he was now attending school but thought that he was most likely attending a unit.

Discussion

These three accounts of Terry's exclusion demonstrate clear differences in how his head teacher, Terry and his mother viewed the appropriateness of the exclusion. His head teacher talked about how she 'had no alternative' and later the school governors 'had no choice' but to exclude Terry. It is uncertain as to whether the head teacher considered that the governors had no choice because Terry's mother had not attended the governors' meeting, or whether Terry's behaviour left them with no choice but to exclude him. There does seem to be a general agreement that Terry's behaviour was more a series of constant irritants over a long period of time rather than serious incidents, with the head teacher explaining that the school had 'come to the end of our patience'. Terry's mother constantly referred to the school's complaints as being 'petty' and 'trivial', and Terry felt that he had not been involved in any serious incident at school, such as fighting or swearing at a teacher.

Terry and his head teacher both spontaneously raised the fact that they thought that the fact that Terry is a black pupil had no bearing on his exclusion from school. His mother had made no reference to Terry's colour. Terry and his mother both referred to how upset Terry felt about his exclusion and had both acknowledged how angry Terry's mother had felt. Neither felt that they had received any help and thought that the support which the school had provided (the school counsellor and the educational psychologist) had not been helpful. The head teacher felt that the school had provided a great deal of help which Terry had 'not taken full advantage of'. With respect to the governors' meeting, Terry's mother was clear that she had felt so angry that her attendance would have made no difference.

There is a sense in Terry and his mother's stories that they believed that there had been no one to help them and that, although Terry felt that there had been a couple of teachers who had supported him, these teachers had not had enough 'power' in the school to help him. Terry seemed not to blame these teachers but rather to accept their position. Terry's mother had been disappointed that the education authority had not supported or helped her and Terry in a way which she had expected, but that instead they '. . . just support the schools'. Terry's mother also expressed the view that the school had not tried to 'know' Terry, yet in her account his head teacher presented as 'knowing about' Terry.

As in the previous case study there is no sense that the home and the school were able to connect with each other in terms of the impact of each upon the pupil's behaviour. The school was unaware of Terry's family's early difficulties, and even if they had been aware it is unclear what difference this might have made to their understanding of the meaning of Terry's behaviour. Again, here is an excluded pupil who experienced early maternal separation, in this case on more than one occasion; again here is a pupil who demonstrated an external locus of control, poor verbal skills and, through his self-esteem assessment held a realistic view of his own behaviour and scholastic achievement, with a wish to improve.

Jade

Jade is a white, 12-year-old pupil living with her mother and step-father. She had been excluded from school in Year 7. In the cognitive assessment Jade had performed in the low average range for both verbal and performance skills. She had a reading age about three years below her chronological age and had received help from the learning support staff in her previous school. There had been no reference to this when we had spoken with the head teacher of the school from which she had been excluded. She had only recently started at that school and the head teacher had commented on the fact that they had not had a chance to get to know her very well.

Jade had presented a negative self-esteem, particularly with respect to her scholastic and social acceptance self-esteem. This did seem to be a realistic self-view as Jade did have some learning difficulties, and due to several moves of home and school, had not found it easy to establish friendships. In terms of the support which Jade considered had been available to her, she felt unsupported by her teachers, her friends and her parents.

Jade presented an external locus of control. She felt that she had no control over where she would live and with whom she would live, or which school she would attend. Such decisions had been made for her either by her parents, her stepfather or by a social worker and Jade could not remember ever being asked what she wanted. This does not, of course, mean that Jade was not asked for her own views, but that she did not remember being asked, and she certainly believed that her views had not mattered or made a difference.

When we met with Jade's mother we discovered that the family had experienced four of the eight family risk factors. Jade's parents had divorced when she was six years of age. Her mother had moved out of the family home, leaving Jade with her father. She had stayed with her father for about three years, but when father's partner moved in Jade had been told by her father that she would have to move to live with her mother. Jade's mother had been living in temporary accommodation at the time with her new husband and it had not been possible for Jade to live with them. She had then been taken into voluntary care, living in a local authority children's home for about nine months. Although this home had been geographically quite near to Jade's father, she had to change schools. Jade eventually moved to live with her mother and stepfather and had started at her new school only a short time before the incident for which she was permanently excluded.

Jade's mother told us that her first husband had been emotionally cruel to her but that he had been a good father to Jade. She had left Jade to live with him because she had left the family home with nowhere to live and with no money and would not have been able to look after Jade. She had moved away from the area and had thought it better not to contact Jade until she was able to get herself settled. She had therefore been out of contact with Jade for about four weeks after she left. On reflection Jade's mother told us that she thinks that she had been having a nervous breakdown when she had left her first husband. She had been on medication for depression and had at one time been suicidal. She had spent a couple of days in hospital having taken an overdose, and had been able to see a counsellor for a period

of a few months. She had now remarried, but told us that her husband had not wanted children and was not used to them. He had not
wanted Jade to live with them but had eventually agreed to her moving in. Jade's mother told us that Jade and her stepfather seemed to
be getting along well but that it was early days, and the exclusion
from school 'had not helped'. She felt that Jade had been trying hard
to be quiet and well behaved around the house so as not to upset her
stepfather.

In terms of family resilience this family demonstrated a low resilience to family risk factors. Jade and her mother were able to tell a
coherent story about their experiences but did not have a sound
cognitive grasp of procedures and events, and Jade's mother had
experienced suicidal behaviour. The family had difficulties in responding flexibly to difficult events and the family situation at the time of
us meeting them seemed to be rather vulnerable. Jade was needing to
take care not to upset her stepfather and her mother had told us that
her husband did not want to have anything to do with Jade's schooling
difficulties.

Jade's story

Jade told us that she had not liked the school but said that she had to
put up with it because when she had moved back to live with her
mother no other school had a place. Jade explained that she had
been living with her father but had to leave there because he had a
new girlfriend. She told me that at her previous school she had not
got along very well with other girls so she had not been too unhappy
moving schools. At her previous school Jade said that she had hung
around with girls who were involved with drugs although she said
that she had never taken drugs herself. She described several incidents in her previous school where she had been picked on by other
girls and been beaten up once by them, out of school, at 11.00 pm
one evening.

Jade said that when she started at her new school it had been 'so
nasty'. Other girls ignored her and did not speak to her. She said that
she started to hang around with another girl who the other girls also
ignored. Jade said that the other girls used to bully her and call her
'Essex girl' because she had previously lived in Essex. Jade told us
that other girls pushed her in the corridor and 'nicked' her things.
Jade said that she had reported these things to her form tutor but
that nothing was done about it. Jade then described how she had

taken a sharp chopping knife from the kitchen at home. She said that she did not think about it but, as she was preparing her sandwiches for lunch that morning, she saw the knife and put it into her bag. Jade said that she had not intended to use it or show it to anyone. She said that she thought that she could trust her one friend so she told her that she had the knife in her bag, but did not show it to her. Jade said that she 'just didn't think about it'. Jade told us that she knew that she should not have taken a knife into school but that nobody had told her that she would be excluded for it. She said, 'I just didn't think I suppose.'

Jade said that she could not believe it when her friend had said to one of the boys 'Watch it or Jade will stab you'. She said that this boy then shouted out 'Watch it, she's got a knife' and the whole class heard it, including the teacher. The teacher asked Jade if she did have a knife and she said that she had taken the knife from her bag and given it to the teacher. Jade said that she and her friend had to write a statement to the principal (head teacher) and that her friend had written that the reason that Jade had taken the knife into school was because Jade had thought that her 'real Dad' was going to go into school to kill her. Jade said that she had never even thought this and she does not know why her friend had said this.

Jade told us that she had to sit outside the principal's office and write down why she had taken the knife into school. Jade explained to us that she really did not know why she had done it, but that she knew that the school would not believe her if she did not give a reason, so she made one up. She wrote that she had taken the knife into school because she thought she was going to be beaten up by the other girls. Jade told us that this was not the truth and that even if the girls had beaten her up she would never had brought the knife out of her bag. Jade said that she still didn't know why she did it, but told us that she really had not thought that she would be excluded for good.

Jade explained that the principal read her statement and then telephoned Jade's mother. Jade said that she just sat there and cried. Her stepfather came to the school to collect her and she told us 'I cried all the way home and all that night'. Jade said that she was told by the school that she would have to see a counsellor, but that she did not see anyone. She told us that no one in the school had seemed interested in her and that now she is glad that she does not go to that school any more. Jade told us that she thought that no one was to blame for the exclusion. She said that if she had been the principal she would have given Jade a detention 'and then done a school assembly about knives'.

Jade described that she had felt very shocked when she had been excluded and that now she felt very stupid. She would like to go to another school but she didn't think that there is much chance of that. Jade said that there were no good things about being excluded from school and that the bad things were that 'you get lazy and miss all your education'. Jade said that the school should 'sort itself out' and properly explain the rules, especially to new pupils. Jade said that there were so many rules in that school and that no one is able to keep all of them. Jade said that she thought that her school was 'the worst school in the area and should be closed down'. Jade told us that she was excluded a week before her mother got remarried. She said that she did not want her to get married again but that her mother was going to get married 'whatever'.

Jade's mother's story

Jade's mother explained to us that the school had telephoned her to tell her that Jade had been found with a knife at school. She said that it had taken her quite a long time to get to the school because she had been at work. She told us that when she arrived at the school the principal told her what had happened and had said that 'this is a permanent exclusion and that there is nothing else you can do'. She was told that the rule about knives was in the school booklet and that there was no flexibility in the rules. Jade's mother told us that she didn't remember seeing the school booklet and she was sure that Jade had not seen it either.

Jade's mother said that when they got home she had believed Jade when she said she did not know why she had taken the knife into school. She told us that Jade had only been in the school for three weeks and she was 'amazed' that she had taken in a knife. Her mother said that after the exclusion the school had told her that they had had no problems with Jade and that, until the knife incident, she had been 'the perfect pupil'. She said that she did not think that Jade realised how serious it had been and that the school could have called in the police.

Jade's mother told us that at the governors' meeting she had explained that Jade had had a disturbed childhood and had asked for her to see a counsellor. The governors had agreed to this but nothing had been arranged. Now that Jade has been excluded she has been seen by an educational psychologist who had written a report saying that Jade should attend another mainstream school. We were told that Jade had received no education since her exclusion nine weeks earlier.

Jade's mother told us that she had attended the governors' meeting and had hoped that, given Jade's background, the governors would have been more understanding and given Jade another chance. She told us that the governors had said how serious a matter it was and they had talked about a head teacher who had been stabbed outside his London school (Philip Lawrence). This had made Jade's mother believe that, because other children knew that Jade had taken a knife into school, the governors probably had no choice but to 'expel' her. However, she told us that she still thought that the school could have kept Jade and given her a different punishment. She wished that she had been able to see the educational psychologist before the governors' meeting, as his report had said that Jade needed a 'period of stability'.

Both Jade and her mother want her to go to another school and said that the LEA has been helpful and they were hopeful that another school would be found without too long a delay.

Jade's head teacher's story

Jade's head teacher explained that it had been 'a shame' that Jade had taken a knife into school because 'that and drugs are the only things which result in an automatic permanent exclusion'. She said that she did know about Jade's very difficult background and that was one reason why she had taken her into the school in the first place. She told us that Jade had made a good start in the school and had seemed settled at home with her mother. It had been a 'great shock and disappointment' when she had taken the knife into school. She explained that many other children had known about the knife and that the school had to be 'very strict about these things'.

She told us that the school had not had a chance to get to know Jade very well as she had been in the school for a very short time. She did not consider Jade to be a dangerous pupil and thought that bringing the knife into school had been 'more an act of silliness than aggression'. Jade's head teacher explained that there had been little to discuss at the governors' meeting as it was very clear to everyone that bringing a knife into school had been 'completely unacceptable' and that it would have been 'giving entirely the wrong message to the rest of the school if Jade had not been permanently excluded'.

Discussion

In these three accounts of Jade's exclusion there is no disagreement about the facts of the knife incident. The difference in the accounts of Jade and her mother and that of her head teacher is about whether or not Jade should have been given a permanent exclusion. Jade's mother had hoped that the school would have taken Jade's difficult background into account and had wished that she had received the educational psychologist's report in time for the governors' meeting. However, she also told us said that she understood that the governors probably had no choice but to exclude Jade, as other children had known about the knife.

In Jade's account she had presented as a naive girl who did not know why she had taken the knife into school and had not expected to be excluded. Her mother also said that she thought that Jade had not realised how serious it was to take a knife into school. Her head teacher had considered Jade's action had been silly rather than aggressive, and had told us that had Jade done anything else she might not have received a permanent exclusion, but that taking a knife into school was one of only two things which resulted in an automatic permanent exclusion – the other being the use or possession of drugs on the school premises.

Warren

Warren is a mixed race (white/black African-Caribbean) 14-year-old boy living with his mother and mother's partner. He had been excluded from Year 9. He had been out of school for five months and had received no education between his exclusion and the time when we met with him.

Warren had experienced some learning difficulties at his primary school but his mother told us that as far as she was aware he had not had any difficulties with his work at his secondary school, although he had been in trouble there from '. . . time to time' for his behaviour. Warren performed within the average range for most of the performance tasks of the cognitive assessment but demonstrated poor verbal skills and some reading difficulties. He struggled with the reading comprehension and reading accuracy and told us that he had always had difficulties reading but he had not received any help for this at his secondary school. He told us that he thought that his teachers probably did not know that he had reading difficulties.

Warren also demonstrated low self-esteem in the domains of behaviour, scholastic ability, job prospects and romance, and felt that he had received little or no support from his teachers, a little support from his friends. He thought that he had received the most support from his mother, but told us that although she had wanted to help him she had found it difficult because she hadn't known what to do. He remembered her going up to the school and also trying to arrange for him to move schools before his exclusion, but he felt that she had not known '. . . the right strings to pull'.

With respect to locus of control Warren demonstrated quite an extreme externality. He had mostly blamed his history teacher for his exclusion, but also blamed other pupils and other teachers for difficulties which he had experienced at school before the exclusion. His mother had made a point of telling us that she did not blame the school and that she thought that teachers have a very difficult job. Neither Warren nor his mother had been able to consider things which they might have been able to do differently.

When we talked with Warren's mother about his early experiences and the family history we learnt that the family had experienced five of the eight family risk factors. When Warren had been 15 months old his mother was found guilty of possession and selling heroin. At the time she was a single parent and she had been led to believe that as such, and because this was her first offence, she would not receive a custodial sentence. In fact she had received a lengthy prison sentence and Warren had lived with her mother. Upon her release, she and Warren moved to a home of their own and Warren's father joined them. Warren's mother told us that she did not use drugs again but her partner did, and also suffered from aggressive outbursts and eventually was diagnosed with schizophrenia. He left the home when Warren was eight years of age, since when it has been just Warren and his mother living in the family.

Warren's story

Warren described how he and his friend had been fishing together a few days before the exclusion and that, unknown to him, his friend had put a knife into his bag. At school the next day Warren told us that 'someone' had gone through his bag and found the knife. He said that he had no idea what the knife was doing in his bag but recognised it as belonging to his friend. He said that he did not tell anyone that it belonged to his friend as he 'didn't want to grass him up'. Warren did not know why someone had looked in his bag. He told the school that he had the knife because he had been fishing. He thought that the school had believed him about the fishing but that they said that as no knives were ever allowed in school he would have to be excluded.

Warren then told us about how he had been sent home for one day for the knife incident, and that on the day he returned he and his friends were teasing some girls and 'biting their necks'. Warren then described how his friend had started to 'touch up one of the girl's breasts' and how he, Warren, had bitten another girl's neck. He said that he did not hurt the girl and although she was pushing him off they were all laughing and 'having a joke'. A teacher went over to him, and the girl who his friends had been 'touching up' said that he hadn't done anything, but the girl Warren had bitten had a mark on her neck. Warren explained to us that the other boy did not get into trouble but Warren was sent to the head teacher's room. At the end of that day Warren was sent home with a letter for his mother. He said that he had not been told what was in the letter so he opened it on his way home. He described how upset and angry he was when he read that he had been excluded. He told us that his reading is not very good and he had asked his friend to read the letter.

Warren had given the letter to his mother when he got home and remembered that she had been very angry with him. She had sat him down and told him to tell her the truth. He told us that when he did tell her the truth she had believed him and had then been angry with the school. Warren acknowledged that he had previously been in trouble in the school for fighting. He told us about fighting a boy whom he though we might know, on the first day at the secondary school, because this boy had taken Warren's blazer and thrown it into a puddle in the playground. Warren had got into a struggle with the boy.

Warren said that he had not received any help from anyone at school to stop fighting but he told us that he did not think that the school could help him, particularly outside school, or on his way to and from school, which was when he usually got into fights. He did not think that there was anyone at school who could help him as he thought that none of the teachers liked him. Warren said that he had always been unhappy at that school and wishes that he had asked his mother if he could have moved schools. He thought that his mother had been the most affected by his exclusion.

Warren had been out of school for five months when we met with him and had received no tuition during that time. He was able to give us no good things about being excluded from school, and described the bad things as being bored and having nothing to get out of bed for in the mornings. Warren said that he was really sorry about his exclusion.

Warren's mother's story

Warren's mother told us that Warren has been 'registered hyperactive' and that he had mild epileptic fits when he was younger. He had missed quite a lot of schooling when he was young and he had found it embarrassing when he could not do the work at school. His mother said that she had no criticism of the school and that they had 'probably done their best'. Warren had had 'reading difficulties'. Warren's mother said that he had always been surrounded by adults and he had always been unsure of how to get along with other children. She described how he 'hates younger children around him'.

Warren's mother told us that his head teacher had sent a letter home and had then telephoned her at home. She had felt that really it had been a case of 'boys will be boys' and that there were worse boys than Warren at the school. She reiterated that she did not blame the school and realised how difficult it must be for teachers today.

We were told that Warren had always experienced difficulties with his school work and he had received help in his primary school from a special unit. He had improved a great deal during this time and his behaviour had also improved. The help stopped when he started secondary school and she was told that Warren didn't need the help any more. She said that Warren was embarrassed when he could not do the work but she accepted that there was not much more that the school could have done, except she would have liked him to have seen an educational psychologist as he had at the primary school. She said that if the school's policy was to exclude then she accepted that. She decided not to appeal because the head teacher told her that it would take a year for the appeal to be heard and by then it would be time for Warren to leave school.

Warren's mother also explained to us that she had been told that her address places Warren in a different LEA from the school from which he was excluded and so he cannot attend the local unit. He has been out of school for five months and he and his mother were still waiting to hear from the unit in the LEA where they now live. She has been told that Warren's papers have not been sent on. His mother told us that it was very difficult having Warren at home as he is not tired because he has not done a day at school. She said that she found it difficult to understand what the problems were at school as she had never had any problems with Warren at home. She said that the only time she gets cross with him is about the state of his bedroom; she said 'even the head teacher says he's a lovely boy'.

Warren's mother described to us how she had felt when Warren had been permanently excluded from school. She said that she wept and 'hit the vodka'. She explained that she had overcome a serious drugs problem some years ago and that the exclusion had nearly set her back. She said that she had not known which way to go and blamed herself, feeling that she had let Warren down. When she had gone to the school she told us that the head teacher had been 'really nice' and he had told her that he didn't think that she could have done anything else. She said that it must been 'awful for him to have to tell me' and said that she had 'felt sorry for the head teacher'.

Warren's mother said that she received no help after the exclusion and that she had had to do everything herself. She had telephoned the tuition service and was told that no one would see her until they had received Warren's papers. She would then have to wait for an appointment. She said that she went in person to child guidance which the head teacher had recommended to her, but was told that she had to go to the child guidance service in her own borough. Warren's mother told us that we were the first people to have contacted her about Warren's exclusion, rather than her doing all the 'running around'. She told us that she is living on the bread line and can't afford for Warren to be at home. She would like to be able to send him to a boarding school and for him to come home at weekends, but she said that she has been told that his behaviour is not bad enough. She told us about Warren's friend's fishing knife and about the final exclusion and that the school was 'a bit unfair perhaps'. She thought that the schools don't understand what it is like for young parents and young boys today, and that teachers are 'a bit old and dated'.

She thought that the army would be good for Warren. She is concerned that Warren should not follow her into crime. She said that he has not been in trouble with the police but she does worry that the longer he is out of school the more likely it is that he may get in with the 'wrong kind'.

Warren's head teacher's story

Warren's head teacher described how Warren was 'one of those kids who is always in the wrong place at the wrong time'. He said that he had 'given him the benefit of doubt on more than one occasion'. He recalled that the final exclusion came about when Warren had sexually abused a girl in the school. He had previously brought a knife into school and these two incidents had 'been the last straw'. He told us that 'on paper the incidents looked worse than they probably really were'. He said that whenever he had met with Warren's mother she had always seemed to be supportive of the school and had always said that she did not have any problems with him at home.

Warren's head teacher told us that he had heard something about the family having involvement with the police but he had never been asked to do a police report for Warren so had no reason to think that Warren had been in trouble 'yet'. He felt that Warren probably needed some special help as he did have some learning difficulties. He explained that he had suggested to Warren's mother that she refer him to the local child guidance service but he did not know if she had taken his advice. He had been pleased that she had decided not to appeal against the exclusion. He said that it would have taken a long time and that 'she might well have won an appeal' although he thought that it would not have been good for Warren or the school if he had come back.

Discussion

In the three accounts of Warren's exclusion there seems to be agreement that Warren's behaviour had not been too bad. His head teacher said that he thought that 'the two incidents had looked worse on paper than they probably were' and his mother felt that Warren's 'pinging' of the girl's bra strap was a case of 'boys will be boys'. Warren had not mentioned the bra strap in his account to us and had talked about his friend 'touching up' the other girl and his biting the other girl's neck. He had also described how his friend had put the fishing knife in his bag.

Warren's mother had described how she had 'felt sorry' for the head teacher and that she thought he had been 'really nice'. She seems to be torn in her account between understanding the school and feeling sorry for the teachers, and at the same time feeling that they were describing her son in a way she did not recognise, and feeling that the school did not understand what it is like for young parents and young boys today.

Warren's mother and head teacher both acknowledged Warren's learning difficulties, although this is not referred to by Warren, except where he describes asking his friend to read his exclusion letter because his reading was not very good.

There is reference made to the possibility of Warren getting into trouble with the police in both his mother's and his head teacher's accounts and a sense of expectation from the head teacher who added the word 'yet' to his statement. Warren's mother's reference was in terms of her own criminal record and her worry that the longer Warren was out of school, the more she worried that he may get 'in with the wrong kind'.

Conclusions

These four case studies that we have reported in detail here serve to highlight how complicated it is for the members of any one system to make sense of the position and circumstances of members of other systems. Even where information is shared, for example, where parents have been able to tell schools about difficult family circumstances, it is often difficult for schools to take account of these circumstances in the everyday life and expectations of school. There seems to be a limit to the degree of tolerance possible in schools, which even the most understanding of schools is unable to go beyond – they have school standards to maintain, OFSTED inspectors to satisfy and league tables in which to compete. There is an acknowledgement that children do need some special understanding from the school where there is a particular family crisis, but this seems to be time limited. Once the crisis is seen as passed, children are expected to 'get over it'. Unfortunately we know that the impact of family stresses and risk factors are often chronic, with long-lasting effects.

In our final chapter we will address how each system may not only achieve greater understanding of each other but develop ways in which they can work together more effectively.

Chapter 7

The child, the family and the school

Putting it all together

Introduction

This chapter will bring together the findings of the child, family and school variables as described in Chapters 3, 4 and 5 and address the interrelationships between these three systems. The chapter is organised in three parts to address policy, practice and further research and developments.

The notion of one system impacting upon and influencing other systems is described in some depth in Chapter 2. As described in the discussion sections presented in Chapters 3, 4 and 5, each of the three variables selected for the present study comprise several sub-systems, thus emphasising the complexity of circular causality. The more frequently used 'linear' model ignores this complexity and searches for straightforward 'quick fix' linear solutions to problems. For example, a 'linear' model would prescribe that if pupil A's behaviour can be modified, by reward or punishment, to behave in school, then the unacceptable behaviour will disappear. However, experience shows that such solutions seldom last. Many disruptive pupils respond well to social skills/anger management training programmes and supervised role-play exercises, but once out of the social skills session they are unable to hang on to what they were supposed to have learnt, or to transfer their experiences of the social skills/anger management setting into the real world context.

Policy

In October 1999 at a conference held in London entitled 'Social Inclusion: Pupil Support' organised to launch DfEE Circular 10/99,

Jacqui Smith, Parliamentary Under-Secretary of State for School Standards, said:

> It's an obvious thing to say – but children only get one chance at school. But every day, tens of thousands of children miss out on their education because they are playing truant or have been excluded from school. The consequences for their education are dire. The situation is unacceptable – we cannot just stand by and watch. That is why we are working towards a simple but challenging goal: to raise educational standards for all. This can only happen if children are in school and learning. The Social Exclusion Unit's report Truancy and School Exclusion set out our ambitious plans for reducing levels of truancy and school exclusion by one third by 2002. The keys to meeting this target are early intervention and prevention through multi-agency working and partnership with parents.

Jacqui Smith continued by announcing an initiative to inject £500 million to be available to promote a social inclusion: pupil support grant, intended to be used by schools on activities such as whole school approaches to improve attendance and behaviour. Encouragement was given for schools, LEAs and outside agencies to work together to tackle what Jaqui Smith referred to as 'multi-faceted problems and reduce exclusions and truancy'. The government continues to link truancy with exclusions, despite a lack of evidence to support such a link. There is also a suggestion inherent in insisting upon this link that the strategies which are likely to help those pupils who play truant from school will be the same as those which are likely to help those pupils who get excluded from school. There may be many reasons why pupils play truant, and we are not suggesting that solutions are easy or simple, but it is likely that pupils who play truant without their parents' permission are disaffected with school and vote with their feet. The excluded group is quite different. These pupils, as supported in the present study, are generally good attenders who enjoy going to school and who, again as supported in the present study, aspire to better achieve and better behave (hence their low self-esteem in the behaviour and academic domains). This distinction between these two groups is important when decisions are made as to how to use the £500 million. It will only be money well spent if it is deployed effectively, and to long-term effect. Circular

10/99 set out the law and examples of what the DfEE considers to be good practice on the following:

- pupil behaviour and discipline
- reducing the risk of disaffection
- school attendance and registration
- detention
- proper use of exclusion and re-integration of excluded pupils.

The circular places an emphasis upon early intervention and prevention through multi-agency working, and through partnership with parents. There is a requirement for schools to set out a formal behaviour policy, and to provide pastoral support programmes for all pupils who have failed to respond to a school's normal behaviour standards and interventions. The circular clearly states that pastoral support programmes should not be used to replace individual education plan (IEPs) for pupils with special educational needs, but that schools should incorporate pastoral support programmes into the IEPs, where such children exhibit behaviour difficulties.

The DfES is currently funding a telephone advice line at the Advisory Centre for Education (ACE) for parents who want to know more about the policies and procedures relating to school exclusion. The government, through the Home Office, is also supporting a National Family and Parenting Institute. As yet there is no data available to evaluate how much these initiatives are being accessed or how helpful they are seen to be. The message, however, still seems to be one of only parents need help with children's behaviour, rather than that we all need help to manage children's challenging behaviour. Most of the parents of the present study felt that they would have been able to advise their children's school on how best to manage their children's behaviour if only they had been asked. They reported that they had felt that teachers had not believed them when they said that their children, who were presenting difficult behaviour at school, were well behaved and no problem at home. They said that the teachers held the view that parents were either seeing their children through rose-coloured spectacles, of that they were soft and unconfrontational with their children.

Practice

Given that all parents and teachers were once children, and themselves subject to the within-child, within-family and within-school
variables as they were growing up, their past experiences, as well
as their here and now experiences, affect how they act, react and
respond to circumstances and individuals. The fact that a teacher
may feel particularly responsible and even fond of a particular child,
or conversely feel dislike for a particular child, is likely to be as much
to do with the teacher's own earlier experiences and relationships as
to anything which the child might be doing. A context, personality
or incident may trigger feelings and memories of early experiences,
which may be positive or negative, and a teacher's response will be
affected, often unconsciously.

Similarly parents' early school experiences are likely to affect how
they respond to the teachers of their own children. If a parent's
school experiences were positive and happy, they are likely to expect
that their own children will experience school similarly. However, if
parents' experiences of school were less positive and unhappy, and if
they were fearful of their teachers, they are not only likely to expect
that their own children will experience school similarly, but they may
also expect to be taken back to those early unhappy experiences
themselves when, in their role as parents, they meet the teachers of
their own children. Any anger and resentment which may have built
up since these parents left school may surface and be enacted when,
as adults, they are able to assert themselves with those who represent
the authority and unhappiness of their youth.

Just as children are often described as having high or low self-
esteem, parents and teachers will likewise hold particular views of
themselves in relation to how they would most like to be. As has
been shown in this study, the notion of self-esteem is complex, and
changing individuals' views of themselves is complicated. It is not
sufficient to tell people that they have an inaccurate picture of themselves. An understanding of why they hold certain views of themselves is needed in order to understand and identify the strongest
forces which will influence change.

Where teachers and parents see the positive results of their efforts
to educate and nurture children, they are likely to hold positive views
of themselves with regard to their roles of teacher or parent. Where
their efforts appear to be less successful, and where they receive constant feedback from others to that effect, they are likely to feel less

positive about themselves. One way of dealing with and protecting oneself from these feelings is to shift the blame and responsibility for the failure onto someone or something else – in other words by developing and perpetuating an external locus of control.

In the case of pupils who have been permanently excluded from school the notion of failure for all concerned is strong. Head teachers reported as feeling a sense of failure when they have to permanently exclude a pupil. Parents expressed views that they felt that they had failed as parents and had not been able to do anything for their children to prevent the exclusion.

Baumrind (1967) reported that positive self-esteem is more likely where there is strong and positive communication between parents and children. This might also be the case where communication is strong and positive between teacher and pupil. The present study revealed that the excluded pupils felt less positively than the comparison pupils in respect of the school ethos measure of 'teacher–pupil relations', and in their responses in the support domain, where they described how they did not feel supported by their teachers nor by their parents. Their school ethos responses were supported by their parents and by the lowest status teachers who all rated 'teacher–pupil relations' low in respect of school ethos.

Ricks (1985) linked the development of positive self-esteem with secure attachment, thus linking self-esteem to one of the risk factors identified by Bowlby (1949). There might therefore be some relationship between the excluded pupils' low self-esteem in those domains which related highly to school, their significantly greater experiences of early maternal separation, and their poorer ability to adjust to the demands and expectations of school life. Absence of a secure attachment may be particularly significant in the development of positive self-esteem where relationships are required or where the replication of some of the parental roles is present. For example, teachers take on some of the parental roles, such as the authority role, the adult role, the setting of boundaries role, the moral teacher role. In the domain of 'close friendships' the secure attachment relationship would seem to be important and relevant. In those domains where there was no significant difference between the excluded and the comparison groups the relationship element can be minimal. A possible exception is the domain of 'social acceptance'. However 'social acceptance' might be possible even where relationships are not strong or close.

Baumrind (1967) also reported the development of positive

self-esteem to be related to clarity of rules and the consistency with which those rules are applied. The fact that the present study found the excluded pupils' self-esteem to be low only in those domains which predominately relate to school life and activity requires further enquiry into the links between clarity and consistency of rules in those schools which have the highest exclusion rates, and in the families of the excluded pupils. The findings of the present study show that there was no difference between the highest and lowest excluding schools in how rules are communicated, but it is interesting to note that the only two head teachers who reported no difficulties with ensuring consistency of applying rules were from the two highest excluding schools. The eight other head teachers all acknowledged that consistency is difficulty and even impossible. It may be that the two head teachers who reported no difficulties have an unrealistic picture of what really happens in terms of consistency, but if they have an accurate picture it is interesting to consider how 'consistency' might have been defined.

That consistency is considered 'easy' may suggest that it is seen as being to do with inflexibility and rigidity. There is some evidence in the responses of these two head teachers that this might be the case. In both cases the head teachers referred to 'enforcing rules' and to staff doing things 'properly' as if consistency is to do with doing things in exactly the same way. *The Oxford Dictionary* definition of 'consistency' refers to 'being in harmony, not contradictory, constant to the same principles of thought or action' and 'the state or quality of holding together and retaining shape'. Although they may have shared the same understanding of the definition of 'consistency' as the other head teachers, there is some evidence from the responses of the head teachers of some of the lowest excluding schools that they were able to achieve some degree of consistency ('harmony, not contradictory, constant to the same principles of thought or action'), for example they refer to 'idiosyncratic rules' as being 'inevitable and acceptable to a point' where as the head teachers of the highest excluding schools considered idiosyncratic rules as being 'not acceptable'.

One implication of the more rigid interpretation of 'consistency' is that there may be less opportunity to recognise or acknowledge 'difference'. If there is a belief that all teachers behave in the same way at all times and in all circumstances with respect to discipline and rules, there is little room for pupils and parents to suggest, and be believed, that any unfairness might have taken place, or that the pupils might at any time be unclear as to a teacher's expectations. There might also be no room for flexibility in relation to pupils' or teachers' particular circumstances or needs. This is exemplified in the case of Jade, who was excluded from one of the two highest excluding schools for taking a knife into school. The head teacher had explained to me that Jade is a vulnerable child who was very new to the school and who had a great deal of home difficulties. The head teacher told me that it had been 'a shame' that Jade had taken the knife into school, and that it was a harmless knife which she would never have used, and which she had not even removed from her bag. However, the head teacher reported that 'it is the one thing which results in an automatic exclusion'.

Lau and Leung (1992) reported inconsistent discipline as being related to external locus of control. Nowicki and Duke (1979) link internality of locus of control with parental characteristics of understanding, tolerance, helping and contact seeking in an open climate. These characteristics can be seen as the same as those which Reynolds and Sullivan (1981) describe as being essential for an 'incorporative' school ethos.

Bernstein's (1971) theory of frame refers to the degree of control which teachers and pupils have over what is being taught. Where framing is strong there exists a degree of rigidity, where there is a reluctance to make exceptions when rules are broken. Where framing is weak, the notion of 'difference' and 'flexibility' is acknowledged and teachers feel more trusted to make professional judgements. Thus the notion of 'control' has a place for all stakeholders in the education of children. The link between pupils, parents and teachers with respect to locus of control is strong. Where the excluded pupils presented external locus of control through their responses to the Nowicki-Strickland measure and semi-structured interviews, the responses of their parents to the semi-structured interviews also suggested externality. They talked about blaming the school or particular individual teachers for their children's exclusion, and were not able to present any notion that they, as parents, might have been able to take control of the situation in a way which might have brought about or influenced a different outcome. There was a sense that these parents were reactive rather than proactive, and when they did try to take the initiative, for example, by contacting the LEA, they felt that they were always in the hands of administrators and 'the system'. This sense of impotence and lack of control seems to have been recognised by their children, who described how they felt unsupported by their parents.

In Reynolds and Sullivan's (1981) description of 'incorporative schools', which were found to be the more effective schools, there is a climate where pupils can develop a powerful sense of their own worth and potential for achievement, and where children develop a sense of personal responsibility for their actions and learning. This climate can be seen as one which promotes pupils' development of internal locus of control.

Rabinovitz (1978) demonstrated black children to be more likely to hold external locus of control than white children, and Louden (1977) found black West Indian (African-Caribbean) children living in the UK to be more external. This is important in respect of exclusions from school given the over-representation of black African-Caribbean children in the excluded population. Remy (1983) found no differences between UK white, African-Caribbean and Trinidadian children. The present study did not comprise large enough numbers of participants to conclude significant differences between ethnic groups or socio-economic status.

Rotter (1966) makes a link between cognitive ability and achievement and locus of control. Although in the present study the parents of both groups were not assessed for cognitive ability or achievement, the resilience rating for 'cognitive understanding of events' was significantly lower for the families of the excluded group. The excluded pupils did demonstrate lower scores for cognitive ability and school achievement, and for verbal skills in particular. Gammage (1985) linked poor verbal skills and poor reading skills with external locus of control. Again, the verbal ability of the parents was not assessed in the present study. However, the resilience rating for the parents of the excluded group for 'coherence' was lower than for the parents of the comparison pupils. As explained in Chapter 4, the term 'coherence' is used to describe the ability of family members to put together an account of events in a clear and understandable way – a verbal skill.

The family risk factors which, in the present study, were revealed as being most significant in the excluded group (early maternal separation and serious illness of parent) are circumstances which will have affected all members of the family. When mothers are separated from their children they are likely to feel anxious, unhappy and concerned about what might be happening for their child. In every case in the present study where there had been maternal separation this had not been by choice. Once mother and child were reunited, the relationship needed to be renewed to some extent. The longer the separation, the more difficult this renewing might be. Children are likely to have learnt new rules and routines from their main carer during the separation. This notion fits well with the idea that pre-school children acquire, through their experience of being cared for within a family system, an idea of a bounded set of relationships. Through separation both from mother and from other family members and familiar surroundings, these bounded sets of relationships are likely to become destabilised. Not only might the separation have been painful and difficult at the time, for both mother and child, but the reunion itself might also be painful and difficult. The child may become more clinging to mother, fearing that she will go away again. This can be even more traumatic for the child if a new sibling arrives with mother. The mother may feel torn between meeting the needs of and bonding with her new baby, and getting to know the child whom she had left. In the present study all three of the comparison group who had experienced maternal separation, ranging from two to four months, were separated because of mother's hospitalisation during pregnancy. This was the case for only two of the excluded group. One of the main differences between these children is that all three comparison pupils were cared for in their own homes, with father or maternal grandmothers doing the main caring during mother's absence. In the case of the excluded group only three of the ten children were cared for in their own homes. As already acknowledged, there were no pupils in the present study who were being 'looked after' by the local authority and that this is unusual in terms of the national picture. An explanation has been offered to explain this, but it is important to link the 'early maternal separation' experiences of the excluded group of the present study to the fact that 'looked after' pupils are over-represented in the total exclusion population nationally. An interesting research study might look at the early maternal separation experiences of the excluded 'looked after' population.

When there has been serious illness of a parent again all members of the family are affected. The other parent (if there is one) will be worried and may be emotionally less available to the children in the family. The present study supports the notion that the excluded pupils felt that their parents offered them less support than the parents of the comparison pupils gave to their children. Parents may try to hide the seriousness of the illness in an attempt to protect their children from worrying. Our own clinical experience has taught us that children can be very perceptive, and pick up on the anxieties felt by adults. Where there is a secret, children will take a guess at what the secret is and either think that it is worse than it really is, or think that it is about them. Children might also try to protect their parents from their own worries and emotions, but may not be able to hold on to these worries and emotions out of the home. School may be the place where such emotions are expressed. If teachers are unaware of the family circumstances, or hold the view that children should put such worries out of their minds whilst they are at school, the result for the child can be a complete misunderstanding by others of the antecedence to the acting out behaviour of the child.

Werner (1989) reported that when parents are under pressure themselves they are more likely to be irritated by their children and treat them with less tolerance and understanding. There may also be a link here between how parents behave towards children under pressure and how teachers behave when they themselves are under pressure, either personally or professionally.

The protective factors in families as described by Jenkins and Smith (1990) can be applied to the school context. The protective factor of 'good parent–child relationships' can also apply to good teacher–pupil relationships. This is supported by the inclusion of 'pupil–teacher relations' in the school ethos indicators used in the present study. Jenkins and Smith (1990) also include 'school competence' as a family resilience protective factor, which can be accommodated within the school ethos indicator of 'the learning context'.

Garmezy and Rutter (1985) promote 'at least one adult taking an interest in the child' as being an important family resilience factor, and Werner and Smith (1982) refer to 'intrapersonal qualities' as being protective. These can be applied to the work of Reynolds and Sullivan (1981) who describe 'incorporative schools' as being characterised by 'teachers' positive view of pupils and parents' and the relationship between attitudes and an organisation as being interactional and intrapersonal.

Weiner et al. (1992) refer to how family variables such as parents' values and attitudes to education, affect how children adjust to school life. Rutter and Yule (1970) agree that an important variable in the 'institutional effect' is the level of pupil acceptance which influences the degree to which pupils share the education perspective. Measor and Woods (1984) describe effective schools as being the 'middle ground', where links are made with pupils' cultures and where there is a recognition and valuing of 'difference'.

Reynolds (1996) recognised the importance of parental involvement in children's education and schooling, and 'parent–teacher consultation' is one of the twelve school ethos indicators used in the present study. Henley (1993) included 'mothers' positive experience of school' as being an important characteristic of resilience. Given that, as shown in the present study, mothers tend to take the main responsibility in the family for the education of the children, when mothers have had a poor school experience, they may be less likely to feel able to engage directly with their own children's school and teachers. They may feel uncomfortable attending parent–teacher consultations or joining the parent–teacher association. This can be interpreted by teachers and by their own children as their not being interested in their children's education. In our work as teachers and educational psychologists we have often been aware of teachers who complain that they never get to meet the parents whom they most want to meet. Usually this has meant not meeting the parents of those pupils about whom they are most concerned. Sensitive and reflective approach and understanding of why these parents do not attend parent–teacher consultations might be more productive than assuming that such parents do not attend because they do not care and are not interested in their children's education.

Professionals who work with families and children represent different agencies and have different prime tasks. Teachers represent education and have a prime task of educating children in basic skills within a broad and balanced curriculum. Their prime task has, over the past two decades, become formally more structured and defined, and is now often described as 'raising achievement', with school results and league tables being published publicly. Parsons's (1999) model of the six functions of education (Table 1.1, p. 1) demonstrates the extreme positions which can be taken to achieve common aims. The current political ethos would seem to promote the 'controlling classical approach', with back to basics as a formula. The 'social democratic humanist approach' is likely to suit those children who are most vulnerable.

Social workers represent the local authority and have a prime task of supporting vulnerable adults and children. Their prime task has also been refined over recent years, mainly due to lack of resources, to one of 'protection', with their capacity to work more preventively being eroded.

Educational psychologists represent education, and have a prime task of assessing, supporting and advising the LEA, teachers and parents about children's learning needs. Like social workers and teachers, their prime task too has become narrower, with statutory responsibilities and duties taking over time previously employed for preventative work.

The refocusing and narrowing of the role of these three professional groups has led to frustration with and between the professions, and a lowering of professional morale. This is to some extent supported in the present study by the excluded pupils and their parents, and the lowest status teachers all of whom rated school ethos negatively in respect of 'teacher job satisfaction'. It is anticipated that the roles of each of these disciplines will extend and develop as a result of the recent Green Paper 'Every Child Matters', where inter-agency collaboration is required of all child and family services, including education services and provision.

An important aspect of the present study is the inclusion of a comparison group. Previous studies of excluded pupils (Parsons and Howlett 1995; Blyth and Milner 1996; Hayden 1997) have looked in depth at the excluded pupils and their families and schools. Any comparison of excluded pupils with their peers has been made only in relation to national statistics and assumed normative data. The present study has been able to compare actual excluded pupils with actual non-excluded peers, and has revealed previously unacknowledged similarities between the two groups. This is particularly the case in those self-esteem domains where there was no difference between the excluded and comparison pupils (athletic, physical, romantic, social acceptance and job self-esteem), and in the significance of risk factors and family resilience (where the only significant risk factors were shown to be early maternal separation and serious illness of parent).

An interesting comparison between the excluded and comparison groups is the difference in who gets referred and by whom to educational psychology services (EPS). Although the figures are small, the only two pupils from the comparison group who were referred to the EPS had both been referred by the school, whereas, although two of the excluded pupils were referred to the EPS by the school prior to their exclusion, nine others were referred either by their mothers or by other professional agencies. Given that the excluded group not only experienced behaviour difficulties in school considered to be serious enough to warrant permanent exclusion, but also had significantly greater learning difficulties than the comparison group, it is of some concern that their schools did not refer them for assessment or additional support.

In order to appreciate the contribution which is made by the present study taking account of the three relating systems it may be helpful to consider interventions which might be employed if only one system is considered. The picture which emerges if the within-child variables of excluded pupils alone are considered would be one of excluded children who:

- are disruptive in school, either because they are just naughty, bloody minded and delinquent or mentally ill
- are academically less able and poor achievers
- feel badly about themselves in the school context
- feel unsupported by their teachers and parents
- blame others for their own difficulties and seem unable to change their ways.

Interventions that provide these pupils with greater support for their learning, develop their ability to take responsibility for their actions and encourage their parents and teachers to provide them with greater support will certainly go a considerable way to helping such pupils. However, finding ways of providing pupils (and especially teenagers) with additional support for their learning requires sensitive thought and is likely to be more successful if ways can be discovered to find out from the individuals what kinds of help they would be able to use best. Many young people do not want an adult sitting next to them in the classroom for fear of embarrassment and being teased by their peers. Interventions that build upon the pupils' strengths can be effective and in the case of self-esteem the excluded group demonstrated that there are areas about which they feel positive about themselves. Schools beginning to value such activities is likely to go some way to improving the 'teacher–pupil relations' which the excluded pupils rated negatively in the school ethos measures.

The introduction of social skills and anger management programmes in schools is unlikely to address the pupils' feelings and emotions which relate to home and family circumstances. Young people sometimes share these concerns with teachers and with their schoolfriends who may pass information on to teachers. Those pupils who find it difficult to share such concerns, or whose parents have instructed them not to tell the school of home difficulties, are likely to become preoccupied with them and react either through withdrawal or through aggression towards teachers or other children.

In these cases, teachers report that they are unable to recognise a pattern or reason for the behaviour, with the pupil seeming to behave unexpectedly, irrationally and unprovoked. Parents may be invited to school to discuss the school's concerns about their child. As explained earlier, these parents may feel unable to attend school and meet their child's teachers, and teachers may then view these parents as being disinterested and unconcerned about their child's education.

The picture that emerges if the within-family variables of excluded pupils alone are considered is one of possible maternal deprivation in the early years, and one of families with weak resilience who are unable to support their children when exposed to risk factors. Interventions that offer parents parenting classes, or offer family therapy to address family dynamics and help them to think about how they support each other and make sense of their experiences will be helpful. Engaging families in such work can be challenging, and the suggestion that parents attend parenting classes is likely to be met at the least with apprehension and possible anger. Support for families under stress can be effectively provided, and families are able to strengthen their resilience to stress through family or individual therapy. In respect of excluded pupils, such interventions may help to provide support required by the family which then 'frees up' the pupil from family concerns and preoccupations to a point where there is a greater capacity to learn new skills in the school setting. However, where such interventions are mandatory, such as in the case of court orders, the intervention can be counterproductive. Parents need to have reached a position of wanting and making a commitment to outside help if they are to be able to access and make use of it.

Individual or mother and child work in relation to the early maternal separation might be valuable, helping parents and children to understand their feelings and the reasons for these feelings, and helping pupils to move on to a less stuck position, more able to adjust appropriately to the school setting.

The picture that emerges if the within-school variables alone are considered is one of 'good schools do not exclude and bad schools do exclude'. The temptation to blame schools is great, particularly as it is from the school that the pupil is being excluded, in the same way that when children are excluded from families (voluntarily given into the care of the local authority) blame is often targeted on the family. Interventions are likely to focus upon changes being made in the school, encouraging schools to adopt more of the 'incorporative' characteristics than the 'coercive' characteristics. Certainly a move from a 'coercive' to an 'incorporative' school ethos is likely to provide children with a positive learning environment conducive to learning. However, this alone will be unlikely to protect pupils who, for various reasons of disturbance, anxiety, mental illness or delinquency, challenge the organisation and its members.

In the present study there were three pupils from the excluded group of 20 whom we considered to be too disturbed to be held in the mainstream school context. Of the remaining 17, 14 could have been well provided for within the school had the school been more aware of the pupils' home circumstances, learning needs and early experiences and had they accessed the support services provided to all schools. The remaining three pupils had been excluded for behaviours that their school and parents had acknowledged as being completely out of character, but which fell into the category of 'will result in automatic permanent exclusion'.

The rich picture that emerges from information gathered from all three systems provides a more realistic picture of what is happening for children who move in and out of home and school, taking with them experiences, sometimes positive and sometimes traumatic, from each. By putting together information collected from all three systems, interventions and procedures are likely to be relevant and meaningful to all stakeholders in the whole area of disruptive behaviour in school which results in permanent exclusion. If teachers are aware of and understand some of the tensions and anxieties which pupils are experiencing in their family context, they are more likely to be able to respond sensitively to reactions and responses which pupils might present in the school context. Systemically, the importance of interactions in different contexts is relevant in the home–school context. The application of family therapy techniques to the school context is worthy of consideration. Circular questioning, picking up on themes which emerge from the individual perspectives of the family or school members, identifying dilemmas and providing each member with equal status and power in working together to resolve dilemmas might be helpful. For example, where a pupil has begun to be rude to teachers, to fail to complete work tasks and homework, an obvious starting point would be for the teacher to ask the pupil what might be happening. At present, the 'asking' often takes the form of a criticism. The 'asking' itself can be a powerful intervention and needs to take the form of curiosity and an enquiry. The tone of the enquiry and the accompanying non-verbal behaviour is crucial in terms of how the pupil receives and responds to the request. In some sense, teachers developing and holding on to an unconditional positive regard for their pupils is likely to facilitate a non-judgemental enquiry when things seem not to be going well for a pupil in school.

A better understanding by teachers that pupils who have poorly developed verbal skills are unlikely to be able to provide teachers with articulate and coherent reasons for their behaviour might also be helpful. Such pupils often respond with mumbles and grunts, or phases such as 'I dunno'. The teacher who understands the pupil's limitations will take account of these difficulties and will be less likely to interpret the response as being rude or insolent. By starting with the premise that all behaviour is for a reason, the curious teacher will strive to understand behaviour.

A greater understanding of the development of 'adolescence' will help many teachers to recognise the necessary challenging of adult authority and rites of passage which all teenagers need to experience. Again, there are implications here for teacher training, both initial and professional development opportunities.

Parents are perhaps more likely to hold unconditional positive regard for their children. When their children present challenging behaviour many parents are likely to ask their children what else is happening for them: are they being bullied? are they in trouble at school? can they do the work? Again, articulate children can explain what is happening and how they feel, but those who struggle to find the words will need more sensitive help to express their feelings. This relates to the systemic emphasis on meanings: what does it mean when a pupil grunts a response to what the teacher or parent believes to be a perfectly clear and reasonable question? It might mean many things – that the pupil is being deliberately evasive – and if so why? It might mean that the pupil is not in touch with personal feelings and is unable to answer the question.

Where families and/or schools are 'closed' systems, in that they set up barriers with the external environment, and where the values, beliefs and ethos of the 'closed' system are different from parallel systems, children are likely to face dilemmas, as they move constantly between the two. Thus conflicts and tensions may emerge. Where families and/or schools are 'open' systems, in that they engage in a continuous exchange with the environment, even where the two systems are different, there is likely to be an acknowledgement and awareness of the difference, and of the potential for tension and conflict. Teachers and parents in 'open' systems will be more able to help pupils to think about the expectations of the different systems and to contain anxieties which may arise. Members who make up systems – in practice this can be the teachers, pupils and ancillary staff – bring their 'outside school' experiences into the school context. In a family this can be the adults and children in the family bringing their 'outside family' experiences back into the home. The 'open' system will embrace these different experiences. The more coercive ethos of the highest excluding schools in the present study presented as being 'closed' systems, where pupils and teachers were required to modify their behaviour exclusively to rules decided upon by the most senior members of the hierarchy. This can be seen as reducing, rather than understanding, the complexities of difference.

The notion of a reductionist approach to solving problems can be seen in the most recent attempts to reduce permanent exclusions from school. Targets have been set. 'Interventions' such as providing separate classes or units for excluded pupils in the same building as the mainstream school is seen as bringing down the numbers of excluded pupils. However, 'exclusion' is more than where one is physically located. A pupil can be in the same classroom as other pupils yet excluded from a particular activity or opportunity.

The concept of equilibrium or maintaining the status quo is relevant to school exclusion and school ethos. By asking the question 'In whose interest is it to reduce school exclusions?' we can consider each member of the system. Disruptive pupils and their parents can be seen as having the greatest interest in the reduction of exclusions. In the present study the excluded pupils reported being unhappy about being excluded, of feeling lonely and isolated and bored, and wanting to continue with their education. Their parents, especially their mothers, reported the devastating effects which the exclusion had on their child and other members of the family. They had difficulty with child-care arrangements and were worried about their child's future. Other children and their parents and schools are likely to have the most to lose if exclusions are reduced. Head teachers may consider that some publicity around their willingness to exclude disruptive pupils demonstrates to other parents that this is a school which has high expectations of behaviour, which is well disciplined. Schools that build up such a reputation are likely to look attractive to parents and as a consequence become high in the parental choice rankings. Schools that 'hang on' to troubled children and which then persevere to support them can be seen by other parents as being too

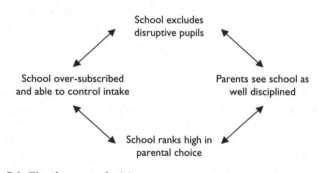

Figure 7.1 Circular scenario (a)

tolerant, so that they decide they do not want their own 'trouble-free' children to attend there. Thus there may be little motivation for many schools to reduce the exclusions of their disruptive pupils. There is perhaps more motivation for them not to admit such pupils in the first place, leading to the following circular scenario, illustrated in Figure 7.1.

Although a school has to send work home for excluded pupils whilst awaiting a final decision to be made, once a school permanently excludes a pupil it no longer has any responsibility for that pupil. Responsibility for the education of the pupil becomes that of the LEA. In the present study only one of the ten head teachers knew what support one excluded pupil had received since being excluded from the school. Consequently it is likely to be in the interests of LEAs to reduce exclusions, and to encourage schools to meet the needs of all pupils within their own resources. The conflict of interest continues and has not moved on from those views expressed by David Hart, General Secretary of NAHT in 1997 and Robin Squire, then Parliamentary Under Secretary of State of Schools, also in 1997, as presented in Chapter 1.

The highest excluding schools can be seen as responding to difficult and challenging situations that feel threatening and unsafe by adopting Bion's (1961) basic assumption or 'role avoidance' level. The managers and teachers in those schools may feel that they do not have the skills or knowledge to work with disturbed and disruptive pupils. Where teachers' and pupils' anxieties are uncontained, an atmosphere of fear and chaos may develop. The quickest and easiest solution can be seen as excluding the most disruptive elements. Another different circular scenario can then emerge, as illustrated in

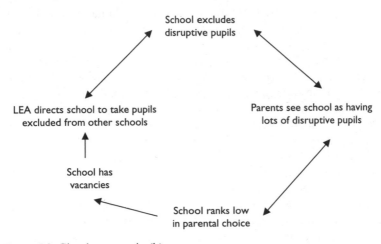

Figure 7.2 Circular scenario (b)

Figure 7.2. Breaking the cycle requires support for the school by the LEA, and possibly a whole LEA policy in relation to excluded pupils moving between schools.

Finally, the concept of 'power' is important in relation to the circumstances of school exclusion. The excluded pupils of the present study and their parents reported feelings of powerlessness and impotence. Pupils reported that where there was a teacher who supported them and opposed their exclusion, these teachers were of low status in the school and carried little influence.

Parents reported feeling powerless in the exclusion meeting which they attended with the school governors. They reported feeling that the school and the governors had already made up their minds to exclude, and that they, as parents, were not able to influence this decision. Excluded pupils reported feeling unsupported by their parents and this can be seen as them recognising their parents' powerlessness to help.

One head teacher told us that sometimes he officially recommended permanent exclusion of a pupil, but told his governors to overrule him at the governors' meeting with the pupil and parents. He justified this by explaining that he wanted the pupil and parents to understand the true seriousness of the situation, and that this really was the last chance. Clearly in this situation the head teacher held the power, even over the governors, who officially held the power in this circumstance. Even when, by adopting a circular intervention where the focus shifts from one of individual blame to one of inter-actions between all parties, where none can be seen as being totally responsible for what happens between them, it should be borne in mind that not all members of the system are equally influential.

What might be learnt from this discussion in relation to how families, pupils and schools can work effectively together to support vulnerable, challenging, disturbed and disturbing pupils within the education system? Given that during the past decade there have been concerns expressed by teachers, parents and government regarding the high numbers of school exclusions, it is useful to consider some of the strategies and interventions which have been suggested and employed to reduce exclusions. An evaluation of behaviour and discipline pilot projects (1996–9) which had been supported under the Standards Fund Programme (Hallam and Castle 1999) reported that successful projects all included eight features:

1   They were established to satisfy local geographical considerations.
2   They consulted and defined needs from the onset.
3   They established effective communication and collaboration with all concerned parties.
4   They involved the whole school staff.
5   They had positive effects on teacher behaviour, enabling teachers to develop a wider range of skills and the confidence to use them.
6   They gave pupils the responsibility for their own behaviour.
7   They gave parents an active role.
8   They developed an understanding of the issues in all concerned.

Hallam and Castle established that the most successful of these projects were those which comprised and worked at a multidisciplinary level. 'Success' was measured in terms of reducing exclusions and cost effectiveness. Multidisciplinary teams were found to cost 40 per cent less than the estimated cost of educating pupils part time out of the school context.

The evidence collected in the present study would support the features which Hallam and Castle identified. However, a greater clarity and attention to detail with respect to some features is likely to result in a greater understanding of what might produce more successful interventions. The need to give pupils the responsibility for their own behaviour clearly, on the basis of the present study, requires some assessment of individual pupils' abilities to recognise that they are responsible for their behaviour. Those pupils who have an external locus of control will require considerably more support and help to move towards a more internal locus of control.

The inclusion of parents as having a valuable role to play requires support and training for teachers in how best to engage parents. In a Standards Fund multidisciplinary project which I set up and managed in a local LEA, the most helpful and valued work identified by teachers and parents was that of the child guidance social worker/ family therapist who was able to model to teachers how to work effectively with parents. The teachers reported how their own communication with parents had developed and become more collaborative, whereas previously they had 'informed parents' and 'advised parents'. Parents reported that whereas they had previously felt badly about visiting the school when their child was in trouble, they now felt more valued and welcomed and more equal with the school. They reported how they had valued the teachers asking for their advice about how they managed their children, and how they had felt that these teachers had really wanted to know how best to work with their child.

Defining needs from the onset of the work is important and not always easy. Systemically it is necessary to acknowledge that different parties will have different needs – a consensus of needs has to be established, a consequence of which might be the need for compromise. A shared understanding of the meaning of behaviour will provide a platform for a shared definition of need. The 'need' might initially be seen as one of 'discipline', but a clearer picture might emerge of one of 'learning needs' – where, as described in the present study, antecedence of pupils' disruptive behaviour was the result of frustration and embarrassment of being unable to do school work.

The identification and 'unpicking' of domains of low self-esteem is needed, rather than an assumption that all pupils who are struggling at school have low self-esteem. This will result in more relevant and refined programmes for pupils. An acknowledgement by schools and parents that areas other than scholastic ability and behaviour are valued and important in children's development is also required.

It might be that the school agrees to focus on support for the family for a period of time, until some stability is possible and the pupil is able to feel contained, less anxious and more able to adjust to the demands of the school context. Such support might take the form of providing a homework club so that homework and its accompanying tensions need not take place in the home, where there may already be tensions of relationships, overcrowding, and so on.

It might be that parents agree to change some of their family routines in order to accommodate some of the needs of the school. Based on the 'resilience' factors of the present study, some parents will need more support than others in understanding some of the routines, procedures and expectations of school. Schools and families may both struggle with the notion of flexibility, defining it as inconsistency.

If, as our study has shown, pupils who are at risk of exclusion from school are more likely to have poorly developed cognitive (especially verbal) and literacy skills, interventions to raise their achievement in these specific areas are likely to reduce children's frustrations and work avoidance strategies. Acknowledgement and the valuing of those non-academic strengths held by pupils is likely to help the lower achieving pupils feel that they do have something to gain from and contribute to the arena of learning.

Helping pupils to develop an internal locus of control, where they can feel a sense of control over their own learning, and over the effects which their own actions and behaviours have over others, will help them to take a greater responsibility for themselves, and how they respond to and are received by others.

By schools including parents in the thinking about their children's academic and social learning, rather than merely informing parents, a more shared approach is likely to be promoted that will prevent the blame culture which often emerges between school and parents when things are difficult.

Easier access to support services such as child guidance and educational psychology, for children, teachers and parents, is likely to help to promote earlier identification of circumstances which lead to vulnerable children finding themselves in vulnerable situations. The setting up of nurture groups for those children whom it is possible to identify as vulnerable at the time when they enter the school system is a cost-effective way of addressing some of the fundamental aspects of deprivation which such children experience.

Easier access to support for families who have experienced major risk events will help them to strengthen their resilience to risk, and will in turn impact upon their own children's resilience to risk. An awareness by teachers that home and school events impact upon children every day, and that school can make a difference, should be encouraged and developed. The present study has highlighted the complexities involved in the interrelationship between home and school and the child's own inner world and resources. Simple solutions are unlikely to find success, and the temptation to look for blame is strong where linear solutions are attempted and found to be unsuccessful.

Further research

As in the case of most research, our study has raised many new questions and ideas for further enquiry. The study might easily have investigated the self-esteem, locus of control and cognitive and literacy ability of excluded pupils' parents and of those teachers involved in the exclusion, or the risk and resilience factors of high excluding schools, the location of 'power' in processes of collaborative work between parents and teachers, and formal and informal power within schools and families. Such investigations would be relevant and informative and might be areas for further study. A greater focus on understanding some of the basic aspects of child and adolescent development in the teacher training curriculum is likely to provide those coming into the teaching profession with a more realistic approach to their work, and provide them with a greater confidence to support those children who present the most challenging behaviours.

Conclusions

This study has demonstrated the mirroring of family and school characteristics. Some children seem innately to possess within-child strengths that serve to protect them from negative forces whatever, but where these strengths are less strong or absent, and where positive characteristics are absent from both the family and school systems, children are likely to be at greater risk, with few characteristics of resilience present to protect them. In these cases children can respond to their circumstances either by withdrawing and isolating themselves, becoming depressed with a potential for mental illness, or by acting out their frustrations through angry, disruptive and sometimes violent behaviours.

Given the interrelationships between the three systems presented in the present study, it will be necessary for members of each system to share their knowledge, skills and understandings, and to take joint responsibility to work together flexibly, with tolerance and sensitivity.

There can perhaps be a no more frightening position to be in, whether you are an adult or a child, of not feeling in control and of not understanding what is happening or why it is happening. Understanding the reasons for such challenging and disruptive behaviours does not serve to condone or accept them. However, understanding is the first step to changing behaviour. If professionals working with children, parents living with children, and children themselves can have a greater understanding of their behaviours, they may feel that they have a greater control in bringing about a change and making a difference.

References

Ackoff, R. L. and Emery, F. (1972) *On Purposeful Systems*, London: Tavistock.

Alder, A. (1964) *The Practice and Theory of Individual Psychology*, 2nd edn. London: Routledge and Kegan Paul.

Anderson, H. (1999) 'Reimaging family therapy: reflections on Minuchin's invisible family', *Journal of Marital and Family Therapy* 15, 1: 1–8.

Antonovsky, A. (1987) *Unravelling the Mystery of Health – How People Manage Stress and Stay Well*. San Francisco: Jossey-Bass.

Association of Educational Psychologists (1994) 'Response to DFE draft circular 10/94', unpublished circular.

Badger, B. (1985) 'Behavioural problems – the primary–secondary link', *School Organisation* 5, 2: 185–93.

Banks, W. C. (1991) 'Are blacks external: on the status of locus of control in black populations', in R. L. Jones (ed.) *Black Psychology*, 3rd edn. Berkeley: Cobb and Henry.

Bar-Tar, D. and Bar-Zohar, Y. (1977) 'The relationship: perception of locus of control and academic achievement', *Contemporary Good Psychology* 2: 181–99.

Bastide, R. (1972) *The Sociology of Mental Disorder*, London: Routledge and Kegan Paul.

Bateson, G. (1958) *Three Points of View*, Stanford, CT: Stanford University Press.

Battle, E. and Rotter, J. B. (1963) 'Children's feelings of personal control as related to social class and ethnic groups', *Journal of Personality* 31: 482–90.

Baumrind, D. (1967) 'Child care practices anteceding three patterns of pre-school behaviour', *Genetic Psychology Monographs* 75: 43–88.

Bee, H. (1989) *The Developing Child*, 5th edn, London: Harper and Row.

Bender, W. N. (1987) 'Secondary personality and behavioural problems in adolescents with learning disabilities', *Journal of Learning Disabilities* 20, 5: 280–85.

Beres, D. and Obers, S. J. (1950) 'The effects of extreme deprivation in infancy on psychic structure in adolescence', in R. S. Eissler (ed.) *The Psychoanalytic Study of the Child*, Vol. 5, New York: International Universities Press.

Bernstein, B. (1971) 'Education cannot compensate for society', *New Society* 15, 387: 344–7.

Bion, W. R. (1961) *Experiences in Groups, and Other Papers*, London: Tavistock.

Blyth, E. and Milner, J. (1996) 'Exclusion from school: a first step in exclusion from society?' *Children and Society* 7, 3: 255–68.

Bowlby, J. (1949) 'The study and reduction of group tensions in the family', *Human Relations* 2, 2: 123–8.

—— (1970) 'Disruption of affectional bonds and its effect on behaviour', *Child and Family* 9, 1: 43–53.

Brodie, I. and Berridge, D. (1994) 'The Exclusion from School of Children Looked after by Local Authorites'. Study Outline. University of London.

Burr, V. (1995) *An Introduction to Social Constructionism*, London: Routledge.

Campbell, D. (1988) *Teaching Systemic Thinking*. London: D.C. Associates.

Cannon, W. (1938) *The Wisdom of the Body*, New York: Norton.

Capra, F. (1982) *The Turning Point: Science, Society and the Rising Culture*, London: Wildwood House.

Carlisle, J. (1983) 'Some relationships between behaviour and learning problems', *Links* 9, 1: 10–12.

Caspari, I. (1976) *Troublesome Children in Class*, London: Routledge and Kegan Paul.

Chandler, L. (1981) 'The source of stress inventory', *Psychology in Schools* 18: 164–8.

Coggins, C. J. (1984) 'A Comparative Study of Locus of Control in Mentally Retarded, Emotionally Disturbed, Learning Disabled and Normally Achieving Students'. Unpublished doctoral dissertation, University of Oklahoma.

Cohen, R., Hughes, M., Ashworth, L. and Blair, M. (1994) *School's Out: The Family Perspective on School Exclusion*, London: Barnado's and Family Service Unit.

Coleman, J. (1974) *Relationships in Adolescence*, London: Routledge and Kegan Paul.

Coleman, J. S., Campbell, E., Hobson, C., McPartland, J., Weinfield, F. and York, R. (1966) *Equality of Educational Opportunity*, Washington, DC: US Government Printing Office.

Collier, R. G. and Jacobson, E. (1987) 'Locus of control measurement for gifted and non-gifted children', *Roeper Review* 9, 3: 196–200.

Conoley, J. C. (1987) 'Schools and families: theoretical and practical bridges', *Professional School Psychology* 2: 191–203.

Cooper, P. and Upton, G. (1991) 'Controlling the urge to control: an eco-system approach to problem behaviour in schools', *Support for Learning* 6, 1: 22–6.

Cooper, P., Smith, C. and Upton, G. (1994) *Emotional and Behavioural Difficulties: Theory to Practice*, London: Routledge.

Coopersmith, S. (1967) *The Antecedents of Self-Esteem*, San Francisco: Freeman.

Coulby, D. and Harper, T. (1985) *Preventing Disruption: Practice and Evaluation in Urban Schools*, London: Croome Helm.

Cowen, E. and Work, W. (1988) 'Resilient children, psychological wellness and primary prevention', *American Journal of Community Psychology* 16, 4: 591–607.

Crandall, V. C. (1973) *Differences in Parental Antecedents of Internal–External Control in Children and in Young Adulthood*, Cambridge, MA: Murray Research Center.

Crandall, V. C., Katkovsky, W. and Crandall, V. (1965) 'Children's beliefs in their own control of reinforcements in intellectual–academic achievements situations', *Child Development* 36: 92–109.

Cullingford, C. (1999) *The Causes of Exclusion: Home, School and the Development of Young Criminals*, London: Kogan Page.

Currie, M. (1998) *Post Modern Narrative Theory*, New York: St. Martin's Press.

Dallos, R. (1997) *Interacting Stories: Narratives, Family Beliefs and Therapy*, London: Karnac.

Davis, H. and Connell, J. (1985) 'The effects of aptitude and achievement status on the self-system, *Gifted Child Quarterly* 29, 3: 131–6.

Dowling, E. and Gorell-Barnes, G. (2000) *Working with Children and Parents through Separation and Divorce*, Basingstoke: Palgrave.

Dowling, E. and Osborne, E. (1994) *The Family and The School: A Joint Systems Approach to Problems with Children*, 2nd edn, London: Routledge.

Duke, M. P. and Lancaster, W. (1976) 'A note on locus of control as a function of father absence', *Journal of Genetic Psychology* 129: 335–6.

Dyal, J. A. (1984) 'Cross-cultural research with the locus of control construct', in H. M. Lefcourt (ed.) *Research with the Locus of Control Construct*, Vol. 3. London: Academic Press.

Elliot, J. G. C. (1993) 'Locus of Control in Children with Emotional & Behavioural Difficulties: An Exploratory Study'. Unpublished Phd. Thesis. University of Durham: School of Education.

Elton, Lord (Chairman) (1989) *Discipline in Schools*, London: HMSO.

Enfield Child Guidance Service Mission Statement (1997), unpublished Mission Statement, Enfield Child and Family Service.

Epstein, J. L. and Komorita, S. (1971) 'Self-esteem success–failure and locus of control in negro children', *Developmental Psychology* 4: 2–8.

Eswara, H. S. (1978) 'Birth order and internal–external locus of control', *Journal of Social Psychology* 104: 145–6.

Findley, M. J. and Cooper, H. M. (1983) 'Locus of control and academic achievement: a literature review', *Journal of Personality and Social Psychology* 44, 2: 419–27.

Fish, M. and Jain, S. (1997) 'Using systems theory in school assessment and intervention: a structural model for school psychologists' in W. Walsh and G. Williams (eds) *Schools and Family Therapy*, Springfield, IL: Charles C. Thomas.

Fisher, L. (1986) 'Systems based consultation with schools', in L. C. Wynne, S. H. McDaniel and J. T. Weber (eds) *Systems Consultation*, London: Guilford Press.

Frick, P. J., Kamphaus, R. W., Lahey, B. B., Laeber, R., Christ, M. A. G., Hart, E. L. and Tannenbaum, L. E. (1991) 'Academic underachievement and the disruptive behaviour disorders', *Journal of Consulting and Clinical Psychology* 59: 284–94.

Friedman, J. and Combs, G. (1996) *Narrative Therapy*, New York: Norton.

Findley, M. J. and Cooper, H. M. (1983) 'Locus of control and academic achievement: a literature review', *Journal of Personality and Social Psychology* 44, 2: 419–27.

Fromm, E. (1956) *The Art of Loving*, New York: Harper and Row.

Galloway, D. (1985) 'Persistent absence and exclusion from school: the predictive power of school and community variables', *British Educational Research Journal* 11, 1: 51–61.

Galloway, D. and Goodwin, C. (1987) *The Education of Disturbing Pupils*, London: Longman.

Galloway, D., Ball, T., Blomfield, D. and Seyd, R. (1982) *Schools and Disruptive Pupils*, London: Longman.

Gammage, P. (1985) 'What is a good school?', *National Association for Primary Education* 1–15.

Garmezy, N. and Rutter, M. (ed.) (1985) *Stress, Coping and Development in Children*, New York: McGraw Hill.

Gillham, B. (ed.) (1981) *Problem Behaviour in the Secondary School*, London: Croom Helm.

Gorell Barnes, G. (1982) 'Pattern and interpretation', in A. Bentovim, G. Gorell Barnes and A. Cooklin (eds) *Family Therapy: Complementary Frameworks of Theory and Practice*. London: Academic Press.

Gurney, R. (1980) *Aspects of School Leaver Unemployment*, Melbourne: Melbourne University Press.

Hall, A. D. and Fagan R. E. (1956) 'Definition of systems', in *Yearbook of the Society for the Advancement of General Systems Theory* 1: 18–28.

Hallam, S. and Castle, F. (1999) *Evaluation of the Behaviour and Discipline Pilot Projects (1996–1999) Supported under the Standards Fund Programme. Research Report No. 163*, London: DfEE.

Halpin, G. and Whiddon, T. (1980) 'The relationship of perceived parental behaviour to locus of control and self-esteem among American indian and white children', *Journal of Social Psychology* 111: 189–95.

Hanko, G. (1994) 'Discouraged children: when praise does not help', *British Journal of Special Education* 21, 4: 166–8.

Harter, S. (1982) *Self-Perception Scales for Children*, Denver: University of Denver.

—— (1985) *Self-Perception Scales for Adolescents*, Denver: University of Denver.

Hawley, D. and De Haan, L. (1996) 'Towards a definition of family resilience: integrating life span and family perspectives', *Family Process*: 283–98.

Hayden, C. (1997) *Children Excluded from Primary School. Dates, Evidence, Responses*, Oxford: Oxford University Press.

Henley, G. (1993) *The Safety Network. Reducing Risk for Kansas Youth*, Kansas: University Press.

Hetherington, E. M. (1991) 'Coping with family traditions: winners, losers and survivors', in M. Woodhead (ed.) *Growing Up in a Changing Society*, London and New York: Routledge.

Hinshaw, S. (1992) 'Externalizing behaviour problems and academic under-achievement in childhood and adolescence: causal relationships and underlying mechanisms', *Psychological Bulletin* 3, 1: 127–55.

Imich, A. (1994) 'Exclusions from school: current trends and issues', *Educational Research* 36, 1: 3–11.

—— (1995) Presentation at BPS and DCP Annual Conference, Warwick University.

Jenkins, J. and Smith, M. (1990) 'Factors protecting children living in dis-harmonious homes: maternal reports', *Journal of Academy of Child and Adolescent Psychiatry* 29, 1: 60–69.

Jersild, A. T. (1952) *In Search of Self*, Columbia: New York Teachers College.

Jobling, M. (1976) *The Abused Child: An Annotated Bibliography*, London: National Children's Bureau.

John, P. (1996) 'Damaged goods? An interpretation of excluded pupils' per-ceptions of schooling', in F. Blyth and J. Miller, *Exclusion from School*, London: Routledge.

Kanoy, R. (1980) 'Locus of control and self-concept in achieving and underachieving bright elementary students', *Psychology in the Schools* 17, 3: 395–9.

Katler, N., Alpern, D., Spence, R. and Plunkett, J. W. (1984) 'Locus of control in children of divorce', *Journal of Personality Assessment* 48, 4: 410–14.

Kendall, P., Finch, A. and Mahoney, J. (1976) 'Factor specific differences in locus of control for emotionally disturbed children', *Journal of Personality Assessment* 40: 42–5.

Kolvin, I., Miller, F. J. W., Fleeting, M. and Kolvin, P. A. (1988) 'Social and parenting factors affecting criminal-offence rates: findings from the New-castle Thousand Family Study', *British Journal of Psychiatry* 152: 80–90.

Lau, S. and Leung, K. (1992) 'Self-concept, delinquency, relations with parents and school and Chinese adolescents' perception of personal control', *Personality and Individual Differences* 13, 5: 615–22.

Lawrence, D. (1985) 'Improving self-esteem and reading', *Education Research* 25: 194–200.

Leach, D. J. and Raybould, E. C. (1977) *Learning and Behaviour Difficulties in Schools*, Wells: Open Books.

Lefcourt, H. M. (1976) *Locus of Control: Current Trends in Theory and Research*, Hillsdale, NJ: Lawrence Erlbaum Associates, Inc.

——— (1982) *Locus of Control: Current Trends in Theory and Research*, 2nd edn. Hillsdale, NJ: Lawrence Erlbaum Associates, Inc.

Lerner, R. M. and Spanier, G. B. (1978) *Child Influences on Marital and Family Interaction: A Life-span Perspective*, New York: Academic Press.

Louden, D. (1977) 'A comparative study of self-concept, self-esteem and locus of control among minority group adolescents in English multi-racial schools'. Unpublished PhD Thesis, University of Bristol.

McClelland, R., Yewchuk, C. and Mulcahy, R. (1991) 'Locus of control in underachieving and achieving gifted students', *Journal for the Education of the Gifted* 14, 4: 380–92.

McCubbin, H., Joy, C., Cauble, A., Cournean, J., Patterson, J. and Needle, R. (1980) 'Family stress and coping: a decade review', *Journal of Marriage and the Family* 42: 855–71.

McLean, A. (1987) 'After the belt: school processes in low-exclusion schools', *School Organisation* 7, 3: 303–10.

McManus, M. (1987) 'Suspension and exclusion from high schools: the association with catchment and school variables', *School Organisation* 7, 3: 261–317.

——— (1989) *Troublesome Behaviour in the Classroom*, London: Routledge.

Measor, L. and Woods, O. (1984) *Changing Schools: Pupils' Perspectives on Transfer to a Comprehensive*, Milton Keynes: Open University Press.

Miller, L., Rustin, M. and Shuttleworth, J. (1993) *Closely Observed Infants*. London: Duckworth.

Minuchin, S. (1998) 'Where is the family in narrative family therapy?', *Journal of Marital and Family Therapy* 24, 4: 397–403.

Morgan, G. (1986) *Images of Organisation*, London: Sage.

Morin, J. M. (1983) 'The influence of sex birth order, family size and family level of interaction on locus of control'. Unpublished Doctoral Dissertation, Brigham Young University.

Mortimore, P., Sammons, P., Stoll, L., Lewis, D. and Echo, K. (1988) *School Matters: the Junior Years*. Wells: Open Books.

Mortimore, P., Sammons, P. and Hillmen, J. (1991) *Key Characteristics of Effective Schools: A Review of School Effectiveness Research*, London: London Institute of Education for the Office for Standards in Education.

Nowicki, S. and Segal, W. (1974) 'Perceived parental characteristics, locus of control orientation and behavioural correlates of locus of control', *Developmental Psychology* 10, 1: 33–7.

Nowicki, S. and Strickland, B. R. (1973) 'A locus of control scale for children', *Journal of Consulting and Clinical Psychology* 40: 148–54.

Nowicki, S. and Duke, M. P. (1979) 'The Nowicki–Strickland life-span locus of control scales: construct validation', in H. M. Lefcourt (ed.) *Research with the Locus of Control Construct: Vol. 2, Developments and Social Problems*, New York: Academic Press.

Nunn, G. (1988) 'The relationship between children's locus of control and perceptions of home, school and peers', *Journal of Human Behaviour and Learning* 5, 1: 63–7.

Nunn, G. and Parish, T. (1992) 'The psychosocial characteristics of "at-risk" high school students', *Adolescence* 27, 106: 434–40.

OFSTED (1995/6) *Exclusion from Secondary Schools*, London: The Stationery Office.

Palenzuela, D. (1984) 'Critical evaluation of locus of control: towards a reconceptualisation of the construct and its measurement', *Psychological Reports* 54: 683–709.

Parsons, C. (1994) *Excluding Primary School Children*, London: Child Policy Studies Centre.

Parsons, C., Benns, L., Hailes, J. and Howlett, K. (1994) *The Experience of Excluded Primary School Children and their Families*, London: FPCS/Joseph Rowntree Foundation.

—— (1995a) *Final Report to the Department for Education: National Survey of Local Education Authorities' Policies and Procedures for the Identification of and Provision for Children Who Are Out of School by Reason of Exclusion or Absence*, London: DFE.

—— (1995b) 'The exclusion zone', *The Guardian*, July.

Parsons, C. and Howlett, K. (1995) 'Difficult dilemmas', *Education* 186: 25–6.

—— (1999) *Education, Exclusion and Citizenship*, London: Routledge.

Petterson, N. (1987) 'A conceptual difference between internal–external Locus of control and causal attribution', *Psychological Reports* 60: 203–9.

Phares, E. J. (1976) *Locus of Control in Personality*, Morristown, NJ: General Learning Press.

Pope, A. (1988) *Self-Esteem Enhancement with Children and Adolescents*, Oxford: Pergamon.

Quattrone, G. A. and Jones, E. D. (1980) 'The perception of variability within ingroups and outgroups: implications for the law of small numbers', *Journal of Personality and Social Psychology* 38: 141–52.

Rabinovitz, R. (1978) Internal–external control expectancies in black children of differing socio-economic status', *Psychological Reports* 42: 1339–45.

Reed, B. D. and Palmer, B. W. M. (1972) *An Introduction to Organisational Behaviour*, London: Grubb Institute.

Reid, K. (1982) 'The self-concept and persistent school absenteeism', *British Journal of Educational Psychology* 52: 179–87.

Reissman, C. K. (1993) *Narrative Analysis: Qualitative Research Methods*, Newbury Park: Sage.

Remy, L. (1983) 'Personality characteristics of West Indian adolescents: a cross-national study', Unpublished MSc thesis, University of Manchester.

Reynolds, D., Jones, D. and St. Ledger, S. (1976) 'Schools do make a difference', *New Society* 37, 271: 223–5.

—— (1987) 'The consultant sociologist: a method for linking sociology of education and teachers', in P. Woods and A. Pollard (eds) *Where the Action Is: A New Challenge for the Sociology of Education*, London: Croom Helm.

—— (1996) *Making Good Schools: Linking School Effectiveness and School Improvement*, London: Routledge.

Reynolds, D. and Cuttance, P. (ed.) (1992) *School Effectiveness: Research, Policy and Practice*, London: Cassell.

Reynolds, D. and Sullivan, M. (1979) 'Bringing schools back in', in L. Barton and R. Meigham (eds) *Schools, Pupils and Deviance*, Oxford: Blackwell.

—— (1981) 'The effects of schools: a radical faith restated', in B. Gillham (ed.) *Problem Behaviour in the Secondary School*, London: Croom Helm.

Ricks, M. H. (1985) 'The social transition of parental behaviour: attachment across the generations', in I. Bretherton and E. Waters (eds) *Growing Points of Attachment Theory and Research (Monographs of the Society for Research in Child Development)* 56, 209: 1–2.

Robertson, J. and Robertson, J. (1953) *Separation and the Very Young*, London: Free Association Books.

Rollins, R. C. and Thomas, D. L. (1979) 'Parental support and control techniques in the socialisation of children', in N. R. Burr, R. Hill, F. I. Nye and I. L. Reiss (eds) *Contemporary Theories about Family*, Vol. 1, New York: Free Press.

Rosenberg, M. (1979) *Conceiving the Self*, New York: Basic Books.

Rotter, J. B. (1954) *Social Learning and Clinical Psychology*, Englewood Cliffs, NJ: Prentice-Hall.

—— (1966) 'Generalised expectancies for internal versus external control of reinforcement', *Psychological Monographs* 80, 609 (whole no.).

—— (1982) 'Social learning theory', in N. T. Feather (ed.) *Expectations and Action*, Hillsdale, NJ: Lawrence Erlbaum Associates, Inc.

Rutter, M. (1971) 'Parent–child separation: psychological effects on the children', *Journal of Child Psychology and Psychiary* 12: 233–60.

—— (1975) *Helping Troubled Children*, Harmondsworth: Penguin.

—— (1976) *Cycles of Disadvantage: A Review of Research*, London: Heinemann.

—— (1981) 'Stress, coping and development: some issues and some questions', *Journal of Child Psychology and Psychiatry* 22, 4: 323–56.

—— (1985) 'Resilience in the face of adversity: protective factors and resistance to psychiatric disorder', *British Journal of Psychiatry* 147: 598–611.

—— (1988) *Studies of Psychosocial Risk: The Power of Longitudinal Data*, Cambridge: Cambridge University Press.

—— (1989) *Studies of Psychosocial Risk: The Power of Longitudinal Data*, Cambridge: Cambridge University Press.

Rutter, M. and Yule, W. (1970) 'Reading retardation and antisocial behaviour: the nature of the association, in M. Rutter, J. Tizard and K. Whitmore (eds) *Education, Health and Social Behaviour*. London: Longman.

Rutter, M. and Giller, H. (1983) *Juvenile Delinquency: Trends and Perspectives*, Harmondsworth: Penguin.

Rutter, M., Maughan, B., Mortimore, P., Ouston, J. and Smith, A. (1979) *Fifteen Thousand Hours*, Cambridge, MA: Harvard University Press.

Sanders, D. (1990) 'The class struggle: a study of disruption in schools in the Aberdeen area'. Unpublished doctoral thesis, University of Aberdeen.

Schwartz, R. C. (1999) 'Narrative therapy expands and contracts family therapies horizons', *Journal of Marital and Family Therapy* 25, 2: 263–9.

Scottish Office Education Department (1992) *Using Ethos Indicators in Primary School Self-Evaluation*, Edinburgh: Dept of Education.

Sherman, L. W. (1984) 'Development of children's perceptions of internal locus of control: a cross-sectional and longitudinal analysis', *Journal of Personality* 52, 4: 338–54.

Sluzki, C. E. (1998) 'In search of the lost family: a footnote to Minuchin's essay', *Journal of Marital and Family Therapy* 24, 4: 415–17.

Stacey, M., Drearden, R., Pill, R. and Robinson, D. (1970) *Hospitals, Children and Their Families. The Report of a Pilot Study*, London: Routledge and Kegan Paul.

Stirling, M. (1991) 'Absent with leave', *Special Children* 52: 10–13.

Stoker, R. (1992) 'Working at the level of the institution and the organisation', *Educational Psychology in Practice* 8, 1: 15–24.

Stott, D. H. (1981) 'Behaviour disturbance and failure to learn: a study of cause and effect', *Educational Research* 23, 3: 163–72.

Sylva, K. (1994) 'School influences on children's development', *Journal of Child Psychology and Psychiatry* 35, 1: 135–70.

Thompson, C. A. (1990) 'Career expectancies of comprehensive school pupils: relationship between cohort, age, sex, attainment and locus of control belief', unpublished MPhil thesis, University of Manchester.

Tizzard, B. and Hughes, M. (1988) *Young Children Learning*, London: Fontana.

Tomm, K. (1998) 'A question of perspective', *Journal of Marital and Family Therapy* 24, 4: 409–13.

Upton, G. (1981) 'The nature and development of behaviour problems', in

G. Upton and A. Gobell (eds) *Behaviour Problems in the Comprehensive School*, Cardiff: University College, Faculty of Education.

Von Bertalauff, L. (1950) 'The theory of open systems in physics and biology', *Science* 3: 25–9.

Wallersten, J. S. and Kelly, J. B. (1980) 'California's children of divorce', *Psychology Today* 13: 67–76.

Weiner, B. (1972) *Theories of Motivation*, Chicago: Markham.

—— (1979) *Achievement Motivation and Attribution Theory*, Morristown, NJ: General Learning Press.

Weiner, B., White, D. and Woollett, A. (1992) *Families: A Context for Development*, Basingstoke: Falmer Press.

Werner, E. E. (1989) 'High-risk children in young adulthood: a longitudinal study from birth to 32 years', *American Journal of Orthopsychiatry* 59: 72–81.

Werner, E. E. and Smith, R. S. (1982) *Vulnerable but Invincible: A Longitudinal Study of Resilient Children and Youth*, New York: McGraw Hill.

White, M. (1995) *Re-authoring Lives: Interview and Essays*, London: Dulwich Centre Publications.

White, M. and Epston, D. (1990) *Narrative Means to Therapeutic Ends*, New York: Norton.

Wilder, D. A. (1984) 'Perceptions of belief homogeneity and similarity following social categorization', *British Journal of Social Psychology* 23: 323–33.

Williams, S. and McGee, R. (1994) 'Reading attainment and juvenile delinquency', *Journal of Child Psychology and Psychiatry* 35, 3: 441–60.

Wills, D. (1945) *The Barns Experiment*, London: Allen and Unwin.

Wolleat, P., Padro, J. D. F., Becker, A. D. and Pennena, E. (1980) 'Sex differences in high school students' causal attributions on performance in mathematics', *Journal for Research in Mathematics Education* 11: 356–66.

Zuroff, D. C. (1990) 'Learned helplessness in humans: an analysis of learning processes and the roles of individual and situational differences', *Journal of Personality and Social Psychology* 39: 130–46.

Index

Note: page numbers in **bold** refer to diagrams, page numbers in *italics* refer to information contained in tables.